Flowers Are Fabulous

PLATE 1

Diane Love

Flowers Are Fabulous
for Decorating

COLLIER BOOKS
A Division of Macmillan Publishing Co., Inc.
New York

Macmillan Publishing Co., Inc.
866 Third Avenue, New York, N.Y. 10022
Collier Macmillan Canada, Ltd.

Library of Congress Cataloging in Publication Data
Love, Diane.
    Flowers are fabulous
    1. Flower arrangement.   2. Fabric flowers.
I. Title.
SB449.3.A7L68   745.92'2   74-14834
ISBN: 0-02-011770-1

Flowers Are Fabulous is published in a hardcover edition
by Macmillan Publishing Co., Inc.

Printed in the United States of America

Contents

Acknowledgments

The photographer, Carl Roodman and the illustrator, Jody Primoff, have made an essential artistic contribution to this book, and I thank them both for their creative talents and their sincere and patient cooperation.

To my mother and grandmother, Jennie,
who showed me the joy in beauty.

List of Illustrations

PLATE 1. A dramatic white marble center table demands the important plum tulips which give a sculptural effect in this focal area.

PLATE 2. The mellow wood of the settle suits the warm red tones of the cyclamens and anemones.

PLATE 3. Sparkling blue cosmos and orange calendulas are reflected in a mirrored setting.

PLATE 4. *Irises* in gradations of mauve are punctuated by deep purple irises and reflect the purplish cast of the blue and white Imari bowl. Stenciled markings on the petals add interest to each flower.

PLATE 5. A narrow-necked antique Japanese basket is balanced with sprays of mixed bellflowers.

PLATE 6. Powdery celadon poppy leaves and artichokes provide enough bulk to balance with the large mahogany wine cooler but do not overpower the subtle style of the Japanese screen.

PLATE 7. The maroon irises in a dark antique Japanese basket are silhouetted against the stark white table.

PLATE 8. Shiny green leaves thicken an assortment of tulips, and the pottery and wood in the room blend with the tulip colors.

PLATE 9. A black Chinese lacquer screen with gold decoration is made more elegant by the display of irises and lilacs massed in a large black container.

PLATE 10. Poppies, columbine, and bellflowers pick up the mood and color of the chinoiserie-decorated urns and the screen reflected in the mirror.

PLATE 11. The strong-patterned Kazak rug and multicolored American basket harmonize with the rust sweet peas, anemones, and calendulas, while the purple bell enlivens the composition.

PLATE 12. The sophisticated combination of coppery leaves, purple irises, and plum tulips is amassed in an oxblood-colored hibachi which stands imposingly in front of a folding Japanese screen.

PLATE 13. The loose-style arrangement complements the tile painting of flowers.

PLATE 14. Speckled leaves enliven the mute coloring of the salmon, peach, mauve, rust to wine flowers and the dusky rose glaze of the pottery vase.

PLATE 15. Full-blown peonies on a piano suggest the large pink magnolias in the Chinese wall painting.

PLATE 16. A low cluster of calendulas, buttercups, nasturtiums, and bellflowers are appropriate with the English ironstone plates and container.

PLATE 17. A sculpturelike arrangement is interesting set in the simplicity and whiteness of this large living room.

PLATE 18. A cozy corner with a skirted table is brightened

with an arrangement of poppies, cornflowers, sweat peas, and eglantine roses which reinforces the flower-patterned fabric.

Author's Note

I hope this book will increase your enjoyment of flowers
and your creative capacity with them. Flowers are the
palette with which I paint. They are the decorative elements I use to create designs. My work with flowers does
not involve botanical study, and it is important for the
reader to understand that this book is not intended to be a
scientific discourse but an emotional and personal account
of how I interpret flowers and react to them. I have used
the names of flowers in the text as a means of guiding the
reader, but my flowers are not exact copies of their prototypes—a feat which I would never attempt. I select the
most dominant characteristics of the natural flower and
exaggerate these qualities in my fabric flowers. Sometimes
I design a flower which incorporates the features of several flowers. I invite you to experience the beauty of my
fabulous flowers, and in working with this new medium,
you will discover a superb means of creating art and an
increased appreciation of real flowers.

I

The Fabric Flower Blooms

The power of flowers! Look what they did for Eliza Doolittle, who became the fairest lady of all. Let me play Pygmalion and make flower arranging an art instead of an effort.

Flowers are familiar to everyone, and yet people are often all thumbs when presented with the job of arranging them. You, at some time, have filled a jelly glass with dandelions or clipped a spray of forsythia and put it into a vase. Why shouldn't you approach the whole subject of flower arranging with confidence? Working with flowers is not the province of a few specially trained people, but something you can do.

My own enjoyment of flowers has evolved into an engrossing vocation from a purely emotional beginning. According to my mother, my love for flowers started when I was a toddler taking my first walk. She told me that I became more excited over a lovely flower garden than I'd ever been over my playthings. By the time I was about twelve my attitude had become more practical, and I wanted to make a career of working for a florist and playing with the flowers. This was a tempting idea but, according to my family, hardly realistic, and it wasn't until after I married and found a sympathetic flower lover in my husband that I began to really fulfill my fantasies. We made weekly excursions to the New York flower market, which offered a myriad of flowers. Sometimes I scooped up irises of every variety. Another week I might be enticed by daisies and snapdragons, but whatever it was, it was always a challenge and a treat to deck the house with boughs of flowers.

Gradually my arrangements took on an oriental quality, influenced by my interest in collecting Japanese and Chinese art. This prompted me to investigate the Japanese method of flower arranging known as *ikebana*, for which there is no western equivalent. The study of ikebana taught me respect for the integrity of the single flower—a basis for any successful flower arrangement.

I guess my love of arranging and gathering things together manifested itself most clearly when I opened an antiques shop, where I sold furniture, accessories, and paintings. Realizing that every setting cried out for flowers, I tried to simulate effects in my shop that one might find at home. But real flowers were out of the question. It would have been far too expensive and time consuming to keep the store filled with fresh flowers. Artificial flowers were the only answer.

Artificial flowers. These words were enough to discourage anyone who had a feeling for flowers, including me.

Plastic Flowers

What does the term bring to mind? I think instantly of plastic poinsettias dispensing fake Christmas cheer in a bank or apartment house lobby, of planters filled with synthetic foliage depressing me still further in the dentist's waiting room. Worst of all is eating real food in a restaurant while looking at a centerpiece of polyethylene plants.

I love flowers, and I know that there are times when nothing can take their place. But, unfortunately, very often real flowers are scarcely more attractive than the plastic variety. What of the tight bunches, already choked and dying, at sidewalk stands? And the tub of anemones at the florist advertised at two dollars a bunch. When a "bunch" is plucked from its companions, it turns out to be four limp blooms hardly able to survive the trip home. And what of the geranium, of the species *Geraniaceae supermarketeriae*, blossoming bravely in its foil wrappings?

Commercial Flower Arrangements

Even if cost is no object and you can afford to order fresh flowers frequently from a flower shop, your thirst for something beautiful may not be assuaged. Most florists, commercially educated, send out arrangements lacking any artistic value. And we, the brainwashed public, frequently accept their mass-produced-looking products even though the bowl of flowers we get is as awkward as an uninvited guest. From birth to death, from wedding to funeral, we are conditioned to give and accept as gifts fresh flowers in unnatural and unattractive forms, like French poodles sculpted out of chrysanthemums or spears of gladioli with carnations, resembling giant pincushions. And because these kinds of arrangements have become standardized, we have lost a vital feeling for flowers. Our emotional responses have withered and we are afraid to make our own choices, to handle flowers, to create something meaningful out of the marvelous variety of blooms which nature gives us. So we give up and allow a programmed response to overwhelm our own innate and individual taste.

I cannot accept this. We must not let the neighborhood florist put us down and pacify us with his standardized, emotionless arrangements. I had to choose a funeral bouquet recently and I encountered just this kind of tastelessness. The florist presented me with his customary selection, geometric shields of gladioli and flat roundels of chrysanthemums, which would have only made this sad occasion macabre. Much to his dismay, I rejected these usual choices and instead gathered up a profusion of heather and white roses, massed them in a round wicker basket, and sent it off as an expression of my feelings.

If fewer buyers were intimidated in flower shops, the "set" pieces that are meekly being bought would soon give way to far more individual and appropriate flowers. These commercial flower contrivances we constantly meet are real flowers at their saddest, and they add little joy or beauty to our lives. We, the public, must demand something better.

Aside from these harsh realities, there are also times when simple economy must be a major consideration. Maintaining a constant supply of fresh flowers in our homes is undeniably expensive. So necessity compels us to admit that fresh flowers are not always a feasible answer to our desire to have flowers about.

Dried Flowers

A partial solution might be the use of dried flowers, but although these can be attractive in the right location, they do not exist in sufficient variety to satisfy every type of interior decor. Also, dried pods, branches, seed heads, and flowers are brittle and difficult to work with, and once assembled must be guarded against the careless guest or playful child who might brush against them. Working with dried materials is an excellent exercise in understanding a very specific kind of flower arranging style, but they just do not have the flexibility needed for general use.

Which brings us back to that loaded term *artificial flowers*. By now it must be apparent that when I speak of artificial flowers I do *not* mean plastic. Instead, I am referring to flowers fashioned from cloth.

Silk Flowers

In my antiques shop I began to experiment with silk flowers. These flowers have been called *silk*, and it is true that early French makers of artificial flowers did use silk as their material. Even the word *silk* brings forth a connotation of elegance and luxury. But I found that flowers made purely of silk had their limitations. When only one material is used, it is impossible to attain the textural nuances and lifelike qualities of all the different types of flowers. In form alone, it is hard to differentiate the subtle characteristics of each flower. Petal and leaf differences disappear, and the flower arrangement becomes an indistinguishable mass of vague shapes which melt together with one flower flopping on another. Because of these deficiencies in silk flowers, I was forced to create a different

The sweet pea's translucent petals are on thin coiled stems. They create a delicate feeling in pale shades of mauve, pink, blue, and yellow and are perfect for low arrangements and as filler flowers.

THE FABRIC FLOWER BLOOMS/3

sort of cloth flower, one which would emphasize more closely the natural qualities which we admire in real flowers. And while these cloth flowers cannot take the place of natural flowers, they can have their own valid place, not as a substitute but as artistic creations in their own right.

With this need in mind, Paris seemed the logical place to go. I knew that for centuries this city had been a center for the making of artificial flowers, and I hoped that somewhere there would be artisans who could put my ideas into effect. I couldn't use the traditional silk-flower makers, who were set in their methods and couldn't accept new ways. But finally I found, hidden away in a dimly lit atelier on the fringes of Paris, people who were willing to execute flower making my way. These women work in nineteenth century conditions, seated at long tables, painstakingly assembling and coloring flowers. After much experimentation and talk with them, I was finally able to achieve the quality of flower I had in mind.

Fabric Flowers

Perhaps it would be interesting to follow the evolution of a cloth flower. Sometimes I decide in advance what flowers I am going to order; sometimes a color or a cloth prompts me to make a flower I hadn't even thought about. Each one is made to my specifications. First I select a material which is right for the particular blossom I have in mind. If it is an anemone, I might use a sized cotton, which will take the strong dyes necessary to get the vivid shades of this flower. Poppies, with their ephemeral, translucent nature, need a single-ply rayon which can be dyed to intense colors but will retain the fragile quality of "poppyness." And sweet peas need sheer fabric so that different

layers of the material can create the different shades of the flower petals (see Plate 2).

I also pick fabric for the foliage and stem of each plant. Anemones have a fringe of leaves at the top of the stem, for which a tube of hollow, rubberized material can be easily manipulated to show the marvelous convolutions typical of anemones. A nasturtium stem is quite different. So for it I will choose a wired paper stem because this better expresses the nature of nasturtium (drawing, p. 6).

This process of selection is carried out with each separate flower. But my choices and decisions are not purely botanical. Of equal importance is my personal interpretation of the nature of the particular flower. Some of the flowers I have made do not have any counterparts; they are flowers of my own invention.

Even if the flowers I choose to have made do exist in nature, my flowers are not always line-for-line copies. Instead, they are like caricatures of real flowers in the sense that certain of their prominent features are accentuated. So my colors are frequently changed to tones which nature has never seen, but which harmonize with other colors to create a feeling or intensify a mood. I frequently alter the scale, too, making flowers either larger or smaller than they would be naturally. I have taken the delicate cosmos and enlarged its jagged, blunt-edged petals to create a bold flower, drawing, p. 8 and Plate 3). These changes don't hit you in the eye, even though they have no prototypes in your garden. The iris actually grows with a stiff, straight stem. But mine have flexible stems, making them versatile (Plate 4 and p. 10). They can be erect or have flowing curves, without losing what makes them an iris. Even foliage may be changed, and leaves might be exaggerated in shape or clustered more thickly

PLATE 2

The soft-textured nasturtium is enriched by its warm colors which shade from deep yellow to tangerine and persimmon, and the rounded leaves provide an excellent contrasting background.

than nature generally allows. These changes are not arbitrary, but the privilege of the artist who takes nature, personalizes it, and makes his own contribution to it.

Having evolved my own kind of flower, I found that my antiques shop was the most appropriate place for its presentation. Customers, seeing the suitability of the arrangements in their settings, wanted to buy the whole look—furniture, flowers, and all. Before long I was in the flower business, but I never forgot that a successful flower arrangement is tied directly to its background.

The need for convincing artificial flowers seemed to have no end. I discovered that there were unlimited commercial, as well as private, opportunities for expanding the use of cloth flowers. When I had the job of creating effective permanent flower displays to complement the promotion of a new cosmetic, I had to prove that my fake flowers would fulfill the same function as fresh flowers and be more practical. And it worked.

Then I was asked to take on the task of replacing the old flower displays that had adorned the European furniture wing of the Metropolitan Museum of Art. What more challenging assignment could I have, for I could reflect in all my arrangements the decorative history of this part of the museum. Working with the finest types of furniture, I became particularly aware of the need to create arrangements which would not be overshadowed by the superb interiors, but would complement them and add a softening touch.

My antiques shop was soon overgrown with blooms. There were arrangements sprouting from every eighteenth century pot, platter, and pitcher. I had to find a new place in which to plant my make-believe posies. So today I have a shop focused on flowers.

PLATE 3

THE FABRIC FLOWER BLOOMS /7

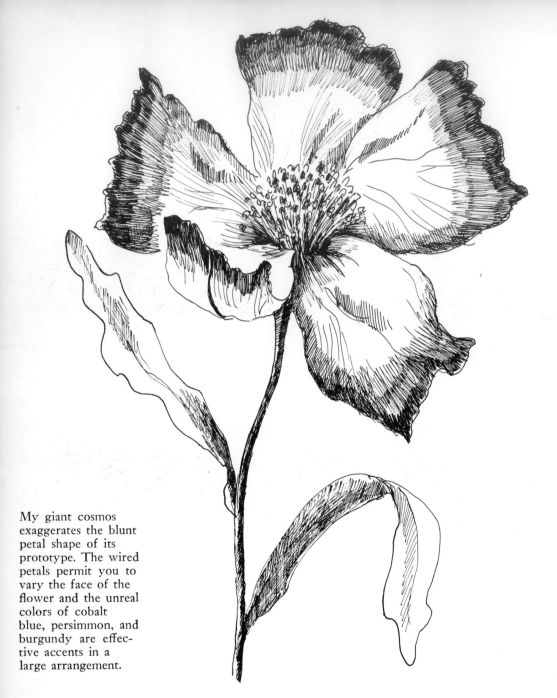

My giant cosmos exaggerates the blunt petal shape of its prototype. The wired petals permit you to vary the face of the flower and the unreal colors of cobalt blue, persimmon, and burgundy are effective accents in a large arrangement.

Every day I discover the unlimited suitability of cloth flowers. They are right everywhere. In my country house, after passing my garden resplendent with day lilies, you encounter as you enter the living room a dappled pot chock full of more day lilies, cloth ones this time. These flowers look right even when you have just seen the real thing. But I always make sure to differentiate between fresh flowers and cloth ones used as a decorative vehicle. Since cloth flowers are totally different from fresh flowers, a mere slavish duplication of nature simply will not work. A woman once asked me to make her an arrangement exactly recreating some fresh flowers in a vase she had recently seen and admired. She wanted, in cloth, a reproduction of the natural flowers she'd thought so beautiful. I tried to explain that although I could produce a facsimile, it would be unsuccessful in expressing the quality of the arrangement to which she had been attracted. The way to bring about a more satisfactory outcome was not for me to copy the original, but rather to synthesize its mood. Thus, to create daisies that look as if they have just been picked from the garden, I must exaggerate. My daisies must compensate for the fact that they aren't real by being fresher than fresh. They must twist and bend, creating wonderful designs. The flowers must be thick in places, loose in others, and also define an interesting and irregular outline around the container. Again, I do this as an artist, who translates reality into an image in order to express his own ideas about nature.

I refer to an arranger of flowers as an *artist* because a successful work of art can only be achieved with a thorough comprehension of the subject being rendered. And I would like to put you at ease and show you how learning to work with both cloth flowers and fresh will

PLATE 4

Tubular stems, blade-shaped leaves are combined with sheer stenciled petals. This ethereal iris comes in every hue of mauve, blue, maroon, and yellow.

heighten your overall understanding of flowers and make you the artist.

Let's take it step by step. I think you will find cloth flowers as satisfactory to work with as real ones. They allow as many liberties as natural flowers because they can be manipulated, clustered, opened and closed, shortened and lengthened at will. They are available in any season and are also, in the long run, more economical than fresh flowers. Most important, when you have created a beautiful bouquet of cloth flowers, it is yours to enjoy indefinitely.

I will illustrate how to select and design a suitable arrangement for any area. One step is to choose a container which will relate to its surroundings and to the flowers in it. The flowers you use and the way in which you learn to arrange them will express your own individuality more accurately than any premade, off-the-counter arrangement possibly could.

I think that too often people minimize the importance of flowers in a room. Art objects, furniture, rugs, and draperies are selected with loving care, while flowers are usually a superficial addition. This is wrong. Flowers represent in microcosm the decor of the entire interior. As such, they are of major importance. Flower arranging is not trivial or pointless; rather, it is a pleasurable occupation.

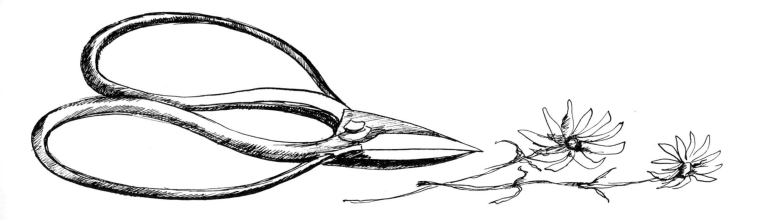

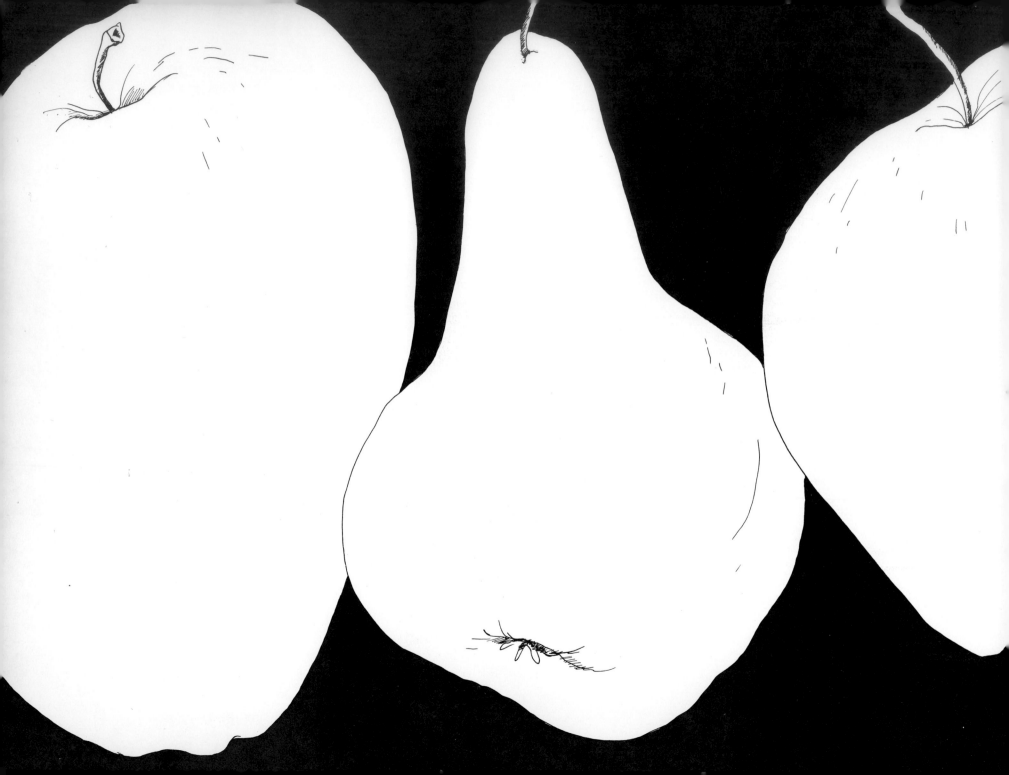

2

The Structured Bouquet

Flowers, like food, should be done with a lavish hand. A basket of fruit toppling with apples is much more appealing than one in which the fruit is gingerly meted out. In almost every case, an oversized arrangement is better and more gracious than an undersized one. This does not mean it must be jammed with flowers. Line, shape, and contour are always vital elements in a successful bouquet.

SCALE

This brings up the matter of scale—an important concept in flower arranging. It is the first problem you must consider when deciding on the new possibilities for flowers in your home. Be careful not to accept the wrong dimensions because your eyes have become accustomed to badly proportioned arrangements. Anything that is different often looks wrong initially, so don't trust your immediate reactions, but be preapred to change to a new frame of reference.

There are two ways in which scale can be incorrect—in the relationship of the flowers to the container, and in the relationship of the whole arrangement to its location. First, let's talk about the arrangement itself. People have come to me with bouquets whose flowers, I would see at first glance, were not in balance with their container. I remember a bowl of roses someone brought to me in which the flowers had been chopped off to form a low mound. The height of the flowers was not equivalent in importance to the dimensions of the bowl, giving it an uncomfortable, truncated look.

It is a well-known rule of thumb in flower arranging that the height of an arrangement should be 1½ times the height of the bowl (see Plate 5). This is a good thing to keep in mind, though as you gain experience you will find that

there are ways of compensating for a change in these proportions so that it need not always be followed exactly. By exaggerating width, for example, or having flowers hanging over the edge of the container, you can sometimes keep height down. A hanging basket can compensate for its lack of height by introducing cascades of flowers over the side. In most cases there is no reason to add additional height to a hanging basket since the attraction of these baskets is the softness and tumbling effect of the flowers.

If you want to use a large planter on a shelf where height is limited, make the arrangement wider and mask the lack of height by having flowers creep over the side. But, one way or another, you must make up for these differences in proportion.

There are also times when the height of the arrangement may exceed 1½ times the height of the container. If you have a massive container of stone or metal of a material which adds to the feeling of solidity, you can use a larger array of flowers than might be used for a container of a more fragile nature, even if the volume of the containers is the same. A tole vase might have too flimsy a look to support a thick mass of leaves, while the same shaped vessel in stone would prevent it from seeming top-heavy. The inverse is also true, and too weighty a container could make an airy arrangement look leaden (drawings, p. 16).

So scaling is the first, elementary step in arranging, and it must be right or the final result cannot possibly be successful.

SCULPTURAL QUALITIES

Anyone familiar with painting and sculpture will be aware of the similarity of method between those arts and the art of flower arranging. Perhaps flower arranging is

PLATE 5

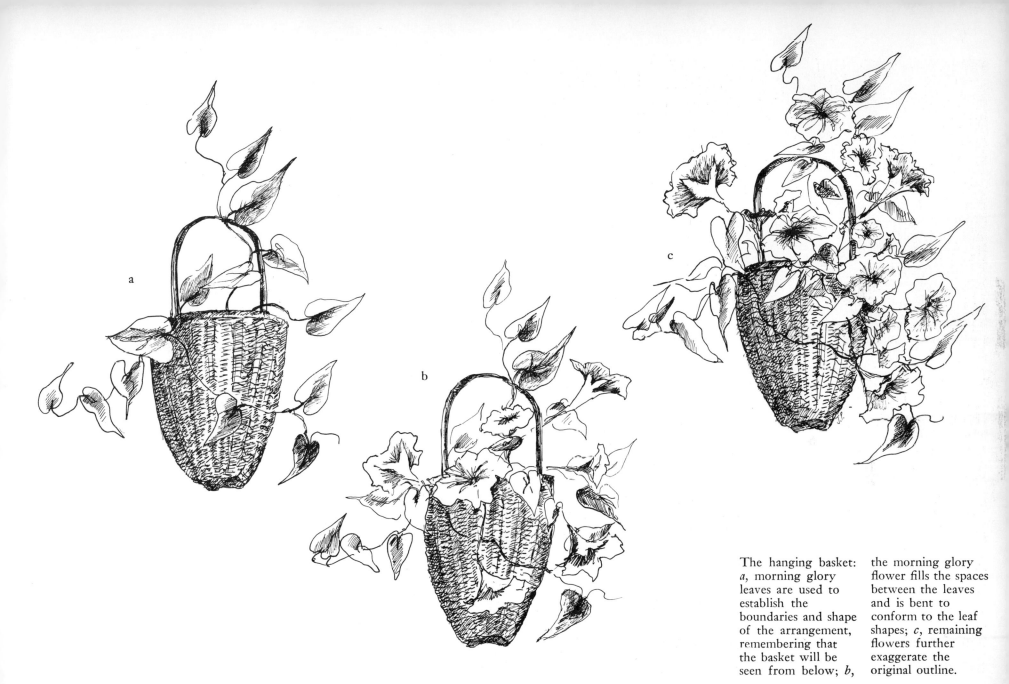

The hanging basket: *a*, morning glory leaves are used to establish the boundaries and shape of the arrangement, remembering that the basket will be seen from below; *b*, the morning glory flower fills the spaces between the leaves and is bent to conform to the leaf shapes; *c*, remaining flowers further exaggerate the original outline.

THE STRUCTURED BOUQUET/15

The identical arrangement is out of scale when placed in an improper container. The basket awkwardly cuts the sweep of the poppies, while the tapering vase extends the movement.

the one simplest and most comprehensive means of understanding many aspects of both painting and sculpture. In flower arranging it is important to have in mind, before you begin, what you are trying to achieve, just as an artist has a preconception of what he is aiming at. This concept might change in the process of execution, but the mind's eye must first have an image from which to build.

Framework

After you have mentally determined your scheme, you then set up the boundaries of the arrangement by placing in the container the highest and widest flowers. With this placement, you will have a framework in which to introduce the rest of the design. If you're using large branches of poppy leaves, it is a good idea to make a skeleton with the branches to create the form you want. Once you have created the dominant shape, introduce the lesser elements. In this instance, the form of the leaves will convey the drama of the entire arrangement (Plate 6).

If a delicate bellflower is going to create a fragile, filmy look, it is wise to establish this outline by first introducing the bellflowers into the arrangement (drawing, p. 19).

When working with cloth flowers, the form and height of the flowers should be set and the flowers shaped before they are inserted into the arrangement. While this isn't possible with real flowers, the cloth ones are capable of much manipulation. The petals, leaves, and stems are all flexible. Each flower's position and attitude should be decided before it is actually put in place.

Positive and Negative Shapes

Flower arranging is closely related to sculpture in that you are working in three dimensions to create a form

The climbing clematis in blue, mauve, and yellow has pointed petals. These are wired so that the petals can be individually shaped to break up the flatness of the flower.

which will be pleasing from all angles. This means that not only the positive shape but also the negative must be considered. By *negative shape* I mean the shape *between* the flowers. There must be a rhythm between the flower elements so that your eye passes smoothly from one spot to the next.

It is easier to arrange flowers in a repetitive, systematic pattern since this is something that we all understand. As small children, our first impulse with objects is to line them up, as we did with our blocks, each one evenly spaced from the next. But flowers done this way will be monotonous. Consciously varying the spaces between flowers when we arrange them requires a calculated awareness of shape—both the positive form of the flower and the negative shape of the space around it. After a while you will see the blandness of an arrangement in which every flower is equally distant from every other flower. There have to be irregular patches of both open and solid areas to carry the eye from one part of the design to the next (Plate 7).

COLOR AS SHAPE

Not only is a flower arrangement like a sculpture; it is really a synthesis of formulas inherent to both sculpture and painting. As in painting, color plays a most important role in flower arranging. While variation of form is vital, the juxtaposition of color is another means of leading the eye from one point to another.

A tangle of red and yellow tulips would be extremely uninteresting if an equal number of tulips in both colors were carefully interspersed (Plate 8). First of all, it is never a good idea to have the same number of flowers in both colors. If you are working with an arrangement in two major colors, such as this, you should use one color at a time, first creating a definite form, then introducing, in the spaces that are left, another form in the other color. It doesn't matter which one comes first because the process is like the meshing of two jigsaw pieces.

When one kind and color of flower is all that is called for, you set up the rhythm by concentrating on the angle of the flowers. Although it is difficult to achieve modulation within one shade, it is not impossible. The color has more impact if the flower is thrust into the center or jabbed at a sharp angle on one side rather than facing obliquely. A grouping of the flower in one spot will also strengthen its color value. In a sense, you are shading the flowers by the way in which you position them (drawing, p. 22).

A slender arrangement of aegean-blue irises in a chrome-finished vase would provide a stark accent in a sleek room. This is when your color sense must encompass more than the arrangement itself; the blue flowers become part of the overall color scheme and are placed there the way a painter

PLATE 6

might use a blue accent to act as a catalyst in a painting. And this is how a one-color arrangement can be used effectively.

A Single Color

Variation and a subtle blending of color are more important in flower arranging than the use of many colors at once. People have a tendency to haphazardly mix flowers of all different colors. When I get a request for a garden variety of flowers in many shades and types, I try to explain that a flower arrangement should make a color statement, and this is impossible if a smattering of every color is introduced. A room should not be a rainbow of colors, but should have one predominant color and some subordinate ones. This opinion of mine is in sharp contrast with the prevailing eclectic taste, which to me is an excuse for a lack of direction. So if you are doing an arrangement in the red family, you will find it much more interesting to include many tones of red, and then perhaps move into the oranges on one side of the color chart, or off into the purples and blues on the other side, rather than many entirely different hues. If you use orangey reds, American beauty reds, fuchsias, and mauves all together, you'll find that the arrangement will work successfully in more locations than it would if it were all one shade of red, since the dominant red in the room will bring out the same red in the arrangement, and everything else will harmonize (see Plates 2 and 11).

Committing yourself to one single shade, whatever it might be, is a much more dangerous method since the color must be right on target. And even if it is right, it will be unimaginative. A flower arrangement is like a pointillist painting in that many colors can combine to bring about

My bellflower (see p. 19) more than any other flower, softens an arrangement and adds a sense of movement with its wispy tendrils. The colors range from yellow, violet, flame red, orange, fuschia, and white.

PLATE 7

PLATE 8

The tulip can be
shaped to any
contour, and these
countless forms
energize the arrange-
ment.

a dominant color effect more vibrantly than if it were done in just one flat tone. A flower array that does blend many tones of a single color will take on the predominant color of the room. If it is an orange room, the orange will be most evident, and so on.

As you do more arranging, your feelings about all these sculptural elements and color nuances will become more defined, and eventually they will be integrated into a style of your own. However, they are not the only considerations that should influence your arranging.

DENSITY

Gradations in the density of the arrangement, for instance, are a factor to think of each time you work with flowers (drawing, p. 23). While there should not be an empty space at the center of the arrangement, if the flowers are equally thick throughout you will lose the sense of dimension. A tangle of daffodils has a heart thickened with entwined leaves and stems, but gradually spreads out so that the outer fringes create an open, irregular web. Delicate bellflowers are clustered at their base and fan out to make a halo of curving stems and dangling bells.

CONTOUR

Shapes must be varied so that a contour is not mechanically reproduced everywhere. If the arrangement is of tulips, their stems should not all be curved the same way. The flat blossoms of the calendula should not all fall on the same plane (drawing, p. 24). And the leaves of a mass of irises should not point in the same direction, nor should those of a nasturtium be slanted at the same angle, creating a flat facade.

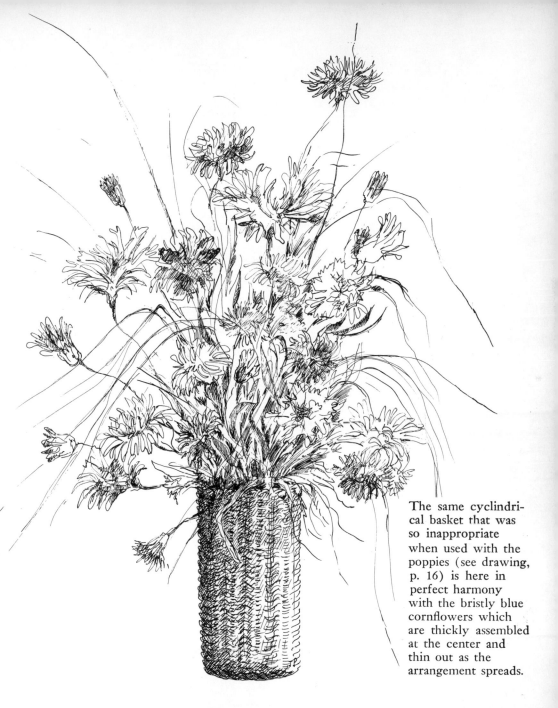

The same cyclindrical basket that was so inappropriate when used with the poppies (see drawing, p. 16) is here in perfect harmony with the bristly blue cornflowers which are thickly assembled at the center and thin out as the arrangement spreads.

The glossy golden
buttercup is a great
accent flower or may
be clumped by itself.

The heads of the
yellow and orange
calendulas should be
tilted at every angle
so the flowers build
more interesting
patterns in the
arrangement.

PLATE 9

TEXTURE

Textural variety is another thing the arranger must have in mind. Opaque cloth must be mixed with translucent. Velvet-petaled pansies contrast well against diaphanous sweet peas. Powdery poppy leaves are exciting when slick, dark green lilac leaves are massed with them as the core of an assemblage of peonies (see Plate 15).

FLOWER FORMS

Variety can be carried right down to the petals and leaves of the flowers. Imagine the roundness of calendulas against the small, satiny petals of buttercups. Clustered sweet william softened with wisps of grass and tumbling morning glories. Each of these flowers provides not only a different texture and shape, but also functions in its own way in the arrangement. The calendulas have tangled stems, while the buttercups stand pert and straight, and the sweet william gives a bunched effect with their many small blooms (drawings, p. 24). Trailers of grass soften it, while morning glories creep in and out among other flowers and tumble over the side of the container. All the disparate elements are woven together into a patterned design.

And again, when you are arranging a group of only one species of flower, with cloth flowers you can take advantage of the flexibility of the petals and leaves. As you saw with the tulips, so a lily is several entirely different forms when it is open, closed, or when the petals are bent in different directions. The angles of leaves turned in different ways create a multitude of interesting shapes. Even by simply making each stem longer or shorter, you are working within the nature of the individual flower to bring about

change. You must constantly concern yourself with varying each flower as if it were the most important one, thinking what twists and turns you can give it to make it unique.

With these basic rules, which will apply to any kind of flower arrangement that you make, we can proceed with an analysis of the specific locations where your bouquets might be placed.

Opposite:
Leaves are as important as flowers. The kind of leaf used, its shape, size, texture, and color is a primary consideration—oak leaf, lilac leaf, straight leaf, poppy leaf.

3

This is the Place

Let's open the front door of your home and walk in.

ENTRANCE HALL

There is probably a console or hall table. Flowers here are particularly important as they are going to convey the first, and therefore the strongest, impression of your house. If the style of the arrangement is inappropriate, the visitor is already misled. For example, a wonderful, large, country-style oak table with an important painting above it would, for me, require a splendid array in a simple pewter, copper, or wooden container. Certainly a dainty little porcelain vase would look foolish in such a setting. A narrow, marbelized ledge in the foyer of a city apartment with limited space needs an elongated container and a three-sided arrangement so that unnecessary flowers at the back

don't push the container away from the wall. If you make your arrangement flat at the back, be sure that you do not create an abrupt line where the flowers end. The flowers must still give the appearance of being continuous. The clusters of flowers must taper off smoothly. It would probably be nice if this arrangement were tall and fan-shaped, for this look is good in front of a mirror or a blank wall. However, a fan form does not mean a monotonously even outline. If one approaches the hall table from one side rather than head-on, the profile of the flowers is of particular importance and must be effective from two different directions, front and side.

Sometimes the entrance table also displays an art object off to one side. It would be interesting to balance this with an asymmetrical vertical arrangement on the other side. But if the emphasis is focused on a central motif, such as a

PLATE 10

THIS IS THE PLACE/29

The two irises and
the grass extend the
simple vase form and
are in balance with
the base at 1½ times
the height of the vase.

clock, a pair of arrangements at either side might be most suitable. When there is enough space, two tables are often used in the reception area. In this case similar but not identical arrangements would be advised. By *similar* I mean composed of the same flowers but with deliberate alterations in the shape and quantities of flowers. Three red flowers, three blue, and so on in each color, would be a bore. The forms should blend but with the main axis of each curving in an opposite direction. They should be fairly high unless there is a specific reason for shorter ones, such as not wanting to hide a painting behind them. A tall lamp on a front-hall table needs a full, low arrangement on the other side to set it off. In the placement of flowers as well as in the creation of the arrangements, you must remember the principles of balance, scale, and variety, which I discussed in the last chapter. The most beautiful arrangement in the wrong spot will never be a success. You can't casually shift your flowers from one place to another and have good results. It's like wearing great shoes with the wrong dress; neither looks right.

Now is the time to go into your hall and look at it with fresh eyes, as if you've never seen it before. Then decide what flowers you can put there to sound the keynote for your whole house.

LIVING ROOM

Although the foyer should suggest the feeling of your home, the living room encompasses your entire decorative scheme. When a guest comes into this room he knows immediately whether the house is streamlined or cushiony, cluttered or spare.

The foyer can only display one grouping of furniture, but the living room is a combination of several, and the

PLATE 11

flower arrangements in these various areas must fit in with the function of the particular spot while also working in relationship to the other flowers in the room as well as the total room design.

Coffee Table

The coffee table, in the midst of a conversation area, requires a low, spreading display of flowers because any flower obstructing the view would be annoying (Plate 11). If there are a lot of small accessories on the table, select a large arrangement. This will break the monotony of many small shapes of similar size. If, on the other hand, there are only one or two large pieces, such as a bowl, an ash tray, or a piece of sculpture, maybe all that's needed is a sprig of something colorful in a vase (drawing, p. 30).

Again, the style of the coffee table will influence the type of flower and container selected. A sleek glass-and-chrome table suggests the trimness of an iris or an anemone rather than a rose or a lilac. And of course these types of flowers should be in a container that plays up the functional lines of the glass and steel. A traditional wooden table needs liveliness to distract the eyes from the expanse of wood. So colorful flowers have to be selected to show up against a somber surface that absorbs the color rather than reflecting it. A rather busy tabletop, with a painted design or mosaic patterns, would look best with a mass of flowers, possibly of one kind and perhaps dark in color so that they are seen as a stark silhouette against the busy background. One extra word of advice when selecting an arrangement for your coffee table: Evaluate whether you want flowers on the coffee table because that is where they will really be most effective or whether you just assume that that spot is best because most people place ar-

The foxglove stalk with feltlike trumpets adds elegance and height.

A pot-bellied pitcher is filled with a thick flower cluster which repeats the round shape of the container. Wisps of grass soften the outline.

rangements there. After all, this table, in particular, is functional; it's used for serving, smoking, magazines, and so on. Perhaps you should consider a location that is not constantly being rearranged, a quiet spot that needs zest.

Sofa Table

The sofa table behind your seating area cries out for flowers. An array here will add a feeling of intimacy and a complimentary backdrop of color to the guests on the couch, and these flowers are not in the way.

Occasional Table

A table at one side of a sofa offers many possibilities for intriguing flower combinations. If the table is against a bare wall create interest with a large vertical arrangement, provided that there is no large lamp already on the table. Foxgloves, bamboo, and cherry blossoms are good for creating this tall line (drawing, p. 32). But if a lamp is important on the table, a small bouquet in a basket or cachepot is more suitable (drawing, p. 33).

Flowers with Paintings

Perhaps there is no lamp, but something of interest behind the table, such as a painting. To complement rather than compete with the painting, there are several possibilities. You can make a low, clustered arrangement, picking up the colors in the artwork but not infringing on its space, or you can style your flowers so that the extending branches are like a three-dimensional continuation of the mood in the picture (see Plate 13). This is more obvious when you have a flower painting and you select similar blooms for your bouquet, but it can also be more quietly

PLATE 12

PLATE 13

PLATE 14

effected with an oriental work, which grows together with the flowers before it (Plate 12).

Dominant and Subordinate Locations

Why do people cling to the idea of giving equal importance to every decorative piece? Just as an actor may "throw away" a line, you must not hesitate to de-emphasize one effect while highlighting another. Partially obscuring one object, by casually positioning another and spotlighting a third will provide contrast and heighten the decorative drama. You are the director and will position each flower display by evaluating its role in the room's design. The greens that you have placed in a tub on the floor will just blend quietly into the background, while the mantelpiece arrangement attracts all the attention.

Since this is true in your overall decor, it is also valid within a single flower arrangement. A woman once exclaimed in horror about an arrangement, "Look! That flower is touching the wall!" My answer was, "Why not?" I explained that every flower cannot be equidistant from the wall. A looser method with flowers provides a change, and frees them from any imagined limitations. It certainly makes the arrangement more natural.

So now you must decide if the flowers you are about to assemble are to be a dominant piece of decoration. Is their function to subtly underscore an important painting or sculpture, to bring out the colors in a fabric, or just to introduce a dot of color in a drab spot? So that the balance of flowers isn't lopsided, some flower displays must be subordinate to others.

Window Location

A table in front of a window always presents a more difficult problem since the background is a changing one—curtains may be open or closed, and it may be daylight or evening. When strong light is coming through an arrangement, you'll need a thicker-looking mass of flowers, as the brightness of the light tends to diffuse the effect. Stems look stemmier and wisps of grass almost disappear. A fragile flower, like a bellflower, tends to get lost against this kind of brilliance. Branches with thickly clustered leaves are a good base for an arrangement in a window location; the leaves will provide a screen against the sun's rays and a background for the smaller flowers (Plate 14), or you can establish a strong form for the arrangement by clustering the flowers at the center. In this way, it won't matter if a little gets lost at the outer edges (see Plate 4). Also, remember that cloth flowers react to sunlight like any

The cabbage-like peony is a majestic form from stem to blossom.

material does. Strong blues, for example, will fade after exposure to constant sunlight, as will other colors.

Some of the same rules applicable to a side table also apply in front of a window. If there's a large lamp, one would not want to have an equally important group of flowers, but if there is no other element of interest on this surface, a splendid array of greens or flowers might be just what's called for. When the table is at the far side of the room it is best to increase the scale of this arrangement and make it the highest in the room.

Large Pieces of Furniture

A very special spot is often on a piano. It's vital that any display on a piano be massive enough to balance with the bulk of the instrument (Plate 15). Voluminous flowers in great array or large leaves generously assembled will work. Any piece of furniture whose size creates a strong decorative effect, like a huge sideboard, pedestaled dining table or marble column, would need as its companion something big to balance.

If a piece of furniture is important, don't assume that its complementary arrangement has to be the focal point. An armoire or a display cabinet may just require something to fill a space between its top and the ceiling. An assortment

of dried material such as statice, or a cascade of greens, can be used, but not a mixture of many kinds of flowers as this would lead the eye to focus on an area which you do not want to emphasize.

Mantel

In England, during the summer, it is a tradition to fill the interior of the fireplace with boughs of greens. In my opinion, although this has been done for centuries, it seems a bit contrived. I would rather decorate the mantelshelf. If there is a pair of objects, such as candlesticks, on either side, then a central arrangement which would fall over the sides of the container and not add a lot to the height would be suitable. But if there's something in the middle, a pair of containers at either end would be advisable (see Plate 10). Sometimes, in extremely informal or modern settings, a balanced group of objects on the mantel is not in keeping with the mood of the room. In this case it's better just to have a basket hanging from the shelf or resting on one side filled with something simple like ferns or cyclamen (drawing, p. 40).

I don't like flowers on shelves. If you have bookshelves or an etagere with art objects and feel you need something, the best thing would be a plant, since there is an

PLATE 15

A network of sweet
green ferns is placed
in a fine woven
basket with sheet
moss pressing through
the basket openings.

Calendula leaves in
a layered form in a
patterned Indian
basket make a thick
green plant set.

The lines that follow were inadvertently omitted from the bottom of the first column on page 43.

on a server. A much more splendid arrangement can be achieved if you're not limited by height for the diners to see over. Otherwise, flowers that are low and tight will have to be used (see Plate 16). Personally I would recommend an important arrangement which would be equally effective on a serving table when not placed on the dining table (see Plate 8). This type of arrangement is attractive as decoration for buffet-style meals. If you feel a permanent dining-table arrangement is best for you, you can

enormous selection of plants made of cloth. Viney effects and exotic varieties are all available (drawing, p. 41).

Now look at your entire living room and determine the combination of flowers you will be using in each arrangement, remembering to create a variety of styles. If, for example, the coffee table has a bowl overflowing just with nasturtiums, perhaps the side table could have an open, airy assortment of flowers. If some other spot requires a filler, foliage would give interest without introducing a totally new decorative element. If there is a bold display of peonies on the piano, an interesting contrast can be made by placing a small, involved-type flower in the same color range elsewhere in the room.

DINING ROOM

In the dining room you are really put to the test of presenting convincing cloth flowers since the dining room table, more than any other area, gets direct attention at close range. The flowers are side by side with the food and so they must not call attention to their artificiality. If you're planning an arrangement on the dining table, you must first decide whether it is going to remain on the table when you are eating or be removed and placed

get some height by using a wispy, open-style flower since this type of flower does not create a solid screen in the midst of the dining table. Of course the shape of the table will decide the shape of your container—oval or rectangular tables look best with elongated vessels. Just for a change, on a long table, you might want to use a pair of containers, one at either end. On a small, circular table something in a square, oval, or round form in proportion with the table is nice. It's uninteresting to always use a round container on a round table, and where variation is possible it should be welcomed. If you have a drop-leaf table which is placed against the wall when there are few diners and opened for guests, you will need an arrangement which is completed on all sides but still will not look awkward up against a wall or window when the table is in its contracted form.

When a buffet or serving table is to be the dominant decorative setting in the dining room, a tall, spreading

PLATE 16

THIS IS THE PLACE/43

Airy narcissus float
out of a round basket,
hanging over the
sides, climbing above
the handle, and
thinning out as they
spread.

bouquet looks beautiful. People are inclined to rely on the dining table itself as the best spot for flowers. I don't agree. Too often a chandelier over the table distracts from flowers below. For a special dinner party when you want flowers on the table, what guest would be unhappy with a flower at his place as a token of a lovely evening . . . bachelor buttons for the men, and sweet peas for the ladies.

BEDROOM

And, finally, the bedrooms. Rules followed in the living room also generally apply here. In all situations, practicality must be considered. Nothing is beautiful if it's in the way or a nuisance. A prime example would be a lavish flower piece on your night table in which you were ensnared each time you answered the phone or turned off the light. A neat little basket, bud vase, or charming porcelain pot would be more attractive.

Every house has some expanse of bare wall which needs enlivening. A large basket, foot bath, or jardiniere set on the floor and filled with branches of specially treated eucalyptus (which lasts for years), woodland ferns, or sleek branches of silk bamboo leaves might fill the void very effectively.

Even in a nursery there is a place for cloth flowers. One of the most successful baby gifts I can think of is a tidy basket of yellow and white narcissus (drawing, p. 44) or a pastel container filled with pink and mauve sweet peas.

We've now gone through every room in your house, and though I do not advocate scattering flowers everywhere, you should decide what your key locations are and put the most beautiful arrangements you can create there. If you're redecorating you will automatically consider new flowers. But even if you're not, you may be surprised at how far some new flower pieces can go toward making your rooms feel fresh, different, and more attractive.

4

Color Counts

When making a selection of colors for an arrangement, you must first decide whether the flowers are to act as an accent, introducing a new color into a room with few or no color accents, or whether the flower arrangement will focus on already established color elements. You might think the introduction of a totally new color gives you unlimited choices, but you cannot just drop a new color into a setting and have it work successfully unless it reaffirms some already established feeling in the decor. The greatest mistake is to think that any color will work in a neutral setting. There are subtleties in every room which, when examined, direct you to the proper color choice.

ROOM COLORS

Too often people think that a beige room with beige carpeting and beige upholstery has no character. But, up-on closer examination, even the blandest decor makes a statement. Ask yourself, is the furniture sleek in its form? Are the decorations angular? Is there an uncluttered feeling? Or is it a room with cushiony, thickly upholstered chairs and many ornamental details? There are colors, just as there are flowers, that definitely convey a feeling of sleekness and modernity. And there are other colors that bring to mind a feeling of traditional warmth.

Neutral Rooms

Here you are, faced with that uncluttered beige room. The colors you choose should have the same direct impact as the style of the room. Vibrant colors, such as pumpkin orange, aegean blue, or Chinese lacquer red might be a good choice in establishing the color emphasis of your flower arrangement. These kinds of colors will not be overpowered by strong shapes of furniture, but will hold their own and supply the proper balance.

In the comfortable, cozy beige room, those same strong colors mentioned before would jolt the eye and bring it to focus on a solitary spot, which is not the purpose of a flower arrangement. Rather, the flowers must epitomize the mood of the room. In this kind of traditional setting, tones of rose, yellow, white, and softer blues would work.

In your desire to provide freshness and color, don't be misled by assuming that the brighter and bolder the look, the more effective and successful the arrangement. Evaluate your room cautiously, making sure that any new addition is still in harmony with the overall mood. For example, an all-white room with beamed ceilings and strong oak furniture would need flowers which provide the same dramatic contrast as the dark wood against the stark white. Tiger lilies, red and orange tulips, or branches of green or russet leaves would carry enough impact.

Now there is the white room with white organdy curtains at the window, and skirted loveseats. Don't shock your visitor with enormous crimson poppies, which create a harsh silhouette against the white. A combination of blue cornflowers, white narcissus, and buttercups would be much better.

A white room with white vinyl upholstery, marbleized floor, and glass and steel accessories requires you to select a color for your flower arrangement that has the same kind of sophistication as the decor itself. There are marvelous black and aubergine-colored silk tulips, maroon irises, and wine and yellow parrot tulips that would hold their own with this strong style (see Plate 17).

Rooms of One Color

You must recognize that the background color of your room does not necessarily indicate the colors of your flower arrangement as much as the style of your decor. Any color—blue, yellow, pink, or gray—when used as the sole color, becomes a neutral element and therefore does not in itself prescribe certain colors for your flower arrangement. It is in a color's relationship with one or more other colors that it functions. Only when you are dealing with a combination of colors do they become catalysts, blending or clashing with other colors. A certain shade of red, for example, can be much more clearly defined when placed against pink, orange, blue, or green. You see immediately if it is yellowish, brownish, or purplish in tone. The quality of redness becomes much more interesting.

An all-blue room doesn't limit you to certain colors because of its blueness. You must determine visually what color or colors would most successfully set off the blueness and make it an active agent. The shade you introduce will create the play of color and animate the background.

You must analyze whether an electric juxtaposition of color, or blending of color, is what you want. Do you want the striking effect of red anemones against those blue walls, or the soft mood of an arrangement of salmon-colored flowers? Reiterating the blue background with a blue flower arrangement would not create a drama of color in your blue room.

Rooms with Patterns

The choice of flowers for an arrangement is much easier when the cast of colors has already been selected.

PLATE 17

A multicolored chintz drapery, plaid fabric, or any patterned and colorful material provides a palette from which you can choose your color flowers. The one key is to make sure you stay within this color group, not whimsically deciding to introduce other colors. It is always easier to work within limitations, and still it is a sufficient challenge to your artistic ingenuity. When given a colorful wallpaper, it is for you to determine which colors you want to be prominent and which colors are to be secondary.

Try for the moment to appraise your fabric or wallpaper from a purely color point of view. If you squint at the material you will better visualize which shades are imparting the major effect in the design, and you will not be misled by the pattern. It isn't always the color covering the greatest surface area that is actually causing the most important stimulus. A material with a multitude of colors like peach, red, orange, and purple may be most effectively coordinated with a flower arrangement if only two colors in the pattern are emphasized—possibly the orange and purple. Even if the orange and purple appear to be of subordinate importance in the design, perhaps when squinting at that same design you will see that those are the colors that are creating the interest (Plate 18).

Rooms with Large Masses of Color

There are many rooms which have a combination of colors where the combination is not represented in any one material. Large, solid areas of color should be related by reintroducing these same tones in your flower arrangement. A yellow room with blue chairs and white-painted furniture could be unified successfully with a combination of yellow and white flowers. It would be much

PLATE 18

50/FLOWERS ARE FABULOUS

trickier, given this already established color combination, to start introducing colors that do not already appear in the room.

When dealing with a combination of large masses of solid shades, the colors in your arrangement must also be determined by the situation of the flowers. Perhaps the color scheme of your room is lopsided and one color seems to be concentrated in a single area. Placing an arrangement of flowers of this particular color elsewhere would help join these two locations.

When combining colors in a room, people are too often at a loss as to how to make the eye take in the entire setting rather than fixing on a particular spot. A flower arrangement is a very easy and pleasing means of tying the room together.

COLOR COMBINATIONS IN YOUR ARRANGEMENT

Whenever you combine colors you are setting up a volatile, forever-interacting unit of color. You can completely change the impact of this unit by adding or eliminating a color.

Blending Colors

If you find that you have assembled an arrangement of flowers that is too harsh in its color composition, the addition of a color may tone it down. For example, an arrangement of fire-engine-red cyclamens and yellow buttercups is hard to absorb visually since both colors pop out at you but do not work together. However, the inclusion of an orange calendula provides the unifying element between the red and the yellow. A simple rule of

PLATE 19

PLATE 20

52/FLOWERS ARE FABULOUS

thumb when dealing with two equally strong colors would be to try to introduce a color which is a mixture of the colors involved (see Plates 2 and 11).

Examples of Unifying Colors:

Combination	Unifying Color
yellow and orange	rust
red and blue	purple
yellow and pink	salmon or tea color
white and red	pink
yellow and blue	tones of green

Softening Colors

There are also situations where the liaison color is not necessarily a blend of the two colors but is like a blotter which helps to absorb hues which might otherwise clash. The liaison color in this case helps to dissipate the impact of two or more very strong colors placed together. For example, glaring orange combined with an equally strong electric blue is brought under control with the addition of a somber purple (see Plate 3). Raspberry and orchid would be similarly toned down by including a powdery, celadon-colored leaf.

Enlivening Colors

On the other hand, sometimes there is a need to introduce another tone to enliven too drab a combination. This new selection must not be so strong that it further deadens the other colors when they are compared to it, but must support the colors of the arrangement. A dark blue-green eucalyptus leaf combined with a dark blue iris is brightened by adding a paler yellowy green leaf, which lifts the effect. Spiky rust leaves subtly combined with purple

PLATE 21

PLATE 22

clematis would be interestingly set off by a few fuchsia-colored leaves (See Plate 19). If you were working with an arrangement of black tulips, your immediate response might be to add a chrome yellow, but the brightness of that yellow would only intensify the quiet of the tulips, and this combination would not make a compatible arrangement. However, with those same black tulips, a spanking white narcissus, which has a touch of yellow at its center, would produce a very crisp result.

Multishaded Flowers

The best means of handling the enormous variety of color is not to lock yourself into any single shade. When I design and select the colors for my flowers I deliberately combine several tones in one flower. The eglantine rose shades from yellow to pink. The strong orange lilium is dotted with dark red. The bright red cyclamen is edged in wine red. The nasturtium shades from pinkish red to orange. Even the nasturtium leaves are toned from green to brown. All of these subtleties enable me to combine a single kind of flower in a variety of arrangements. In this same way you must attune yourself to selecting flowers which will expand the possibilities of your arrangement and thus make it more interesting (Plate 20).

COLOR IN THE CONTAINER

Not only does the container for your arrangement have to harmonize with the setting of the room, but it is equally important that it reflect, in its color, shape, and material, the kind of flower arrangement you are placing in it (Plate 21). Don't ever think that the receptacle for your flowers

PLATE 23

can be disguised or hidden. A pyrex bowl conveys a feeling just as much as a flowered porcelain cachepot.

You will find it more difficult and less successful working with a colorless container, such as glass or silver, because in these cases you cannot re-emphasize your flower selection with the color of the container. You must be sure to link the color of the flowers with their vessel. A green bowl filled with yellow dandelions wouldn't be very successful without the green of the dandelion leaves. This pulls the whole thing together. In the same way a blue-and-white patterned bowl would be lost with any combination of color that did not include even the smallest amount of blue and white.

Basket Color

One of the beauties and pleasures of using a basket is the fact that a basket blends or coordinates more easily with more combinations of colors than most containers do (see Plate 22). The dark brown color of some antique Japanese baskets needs to be repeated in the color scheme of its arrangement. When the arrangement is predominantly yellow, introducing a few maroon irises provides that necessary coordinating dark factor. But not everything works in a basket. The same dark Japanese basket would be awful filled with pink roses.

There are many wonderful baskets that have accent colors painted on them. These details might seem unimportant, and yet this thread of color is an amazing asset when harmonizing the flowers with the basket (see Plate 11), if you are sure to repeat the same color detail. Therefore, if you're eager to use in your arrangement a certain color which you feel coordinates with the decor, your

task will be simplified if you choose a basket, vase, or pot which incorporates this color.

White Containers

Another fallacy is that white is a neutral color, harmonizing with any combination of colors in any color container. This is not so, although an all-white base does

PLATE 24

need to have at least a trace of white repeated in the floral arrangement.

Now that you realize that the color of your container is important, you must further consider the other characteristics embodied in the receptacle, as you will see in the following chapter.

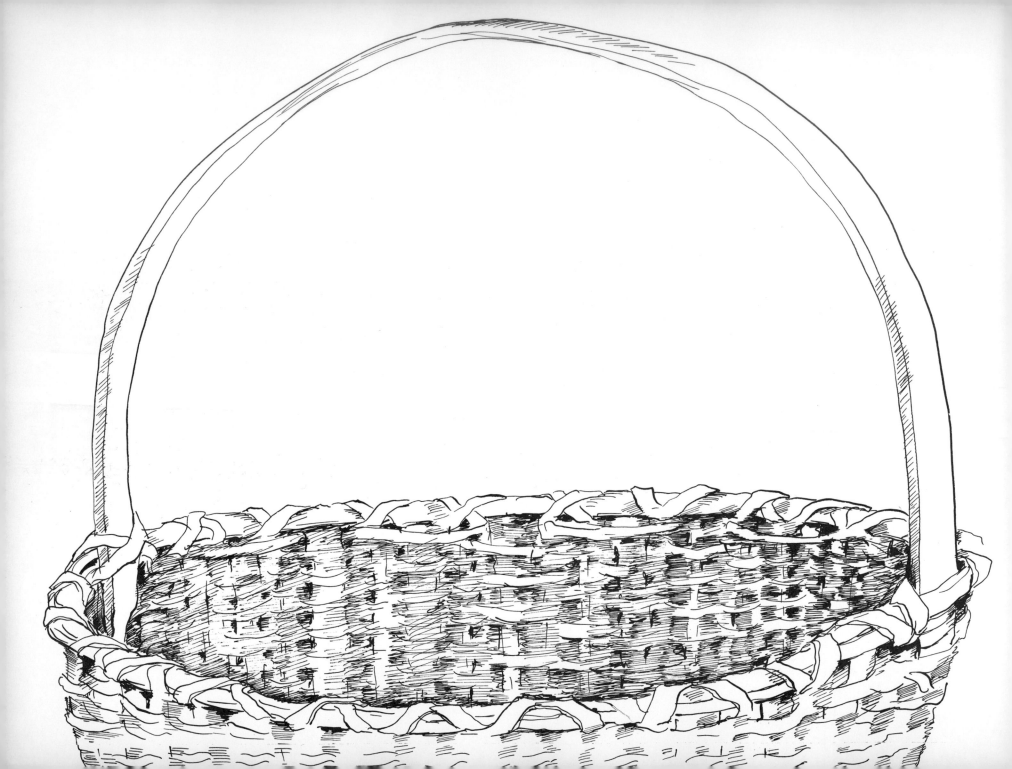

5

The Complementary Container

Think of the container as the legs of your arrangement. It is the support, both literally and artistically, and is an essential part of the whole. Just visualize how foolish skinny limbs look holding up a fat form, and stocky legs with a narrow body.

Every container is a composite of the four following attributes: shape, size, texture, and color. And it is the combination of these characteristics which creates the style of the container.

SHAPE

The shape of the container carries more impact than any of its other characteristics. It expresses the type of structure and direction the flower arrangement must have.

The best way to test the suitability of the shape is to silhouette in your mind's eye the entire outline (flowers and container together), disregarding for that moment the elements of color and texture. You build an arrangement with the idea of exaggerating the form of the container. And it is by further extending the outline of the container that you completely integrate the floral element with its base. If a receptacle flares, the leaves and flowers should enlarge that spreading movement. If it is columnar in form, an upward thrust would extend that straight, vertical line. The bowl shape needs curved and bending flowers to continue the rounded sweep.

The flowers in a winged-swan container should be bent in winglike shapes, carrying out the movement of the swan form. If the same sprays of flowers went in all directions, the flowers could just as well have been placed in

PLATE 25

60/FLOWERS ARE FABULOUS

any symmetrical abstract vase. Flowers in a cornucopia shape should continue the arc-shaped movement of the horn. And a squat container needs a squat, chunky flower.

I was once asked to fill a marvelous, owl-shaped pottery container made by Picasso. It was a whimsical, amusing bird with a stocky shape and simple color. Its form clearly directed my choice of flowers. Just white cyclamens assembled in a thick mass in the opening at the top was enough. The flowers looked like a white tuft on the bird's head and were as unpretentious and direct as the owl.

An antique Japanese basket with a square base is coordinated with a blunt-edge of the cosmos petal (Plate 25).

So it is not only the overall shape of the arrangement that repeats the basket form, but the outlines of the flowers themselves. The more you arrange flowers, the more perceptive you will be in harmonizing these small details.

Shallow Containers

The shallow receptacle, though widely recommended by many English flower arrangers, is not in my mind a very good choice, for in most of these cases the container is so low that the flowers appear to be sitting in a hole. Do not truncate your flowers by using a low container. The head and torso of a figure won't work without legs.

Eglantine roses extend the elongated line of the shallow, rectangular basket.

The only time it is advantageous to use such a shallow container is when the overall height of the arrangement is limited. In this instance you would carry out the low line in the flowers as well, giving sense to the object below. If you are working with a container which is two or three inches tall, pansies or eglantine roses mounded together would be delightful. However, English floristry tradition differs. Sometimes they place the most lavish arrays in the lowest bowls.

Only the Japanese flower master, when working in the ikebana style, successfully uses the horizontal container. In this style of arrangement the surface dimension plays an important part because you see the shape from above. The flowers spring from a small area of the container, and the arms of the arrangement are intended to form beautiful lines against the open dish.

Handles

One other element which gives strength and interest to the shape of an arrangement is the handle, for this projection accentuates most clearly the conformation of the vessel and provides a skeletal structure within which to place your flowers. So do not ever use a handled container with the idea of hiding the handle. If you don't want a handle, look for another vessel, for the handle should be integrated with the kind of arrangement you are making (see Plate 26).

Types of Handled Containers

handled baskets
pitchers
dippers
buckets

PLATE 26

Although the nasturtiums form a tight arrangement, the leaf and flower shapes extend below the rim of the pot and break up the plain surface.

The shape of the Tiffany vase predetermines the style of flower to be used—Easter lily, lilium, iris, or tulip.

THE COMPLEMENTARY CONTAINER/63

SIZE

An awareness of each design factor strengthens the whole, so once you have established the outline of your arrangement you must align the size of the container with its contents. Identically shaped containers in different sizes require different kinds of flowers to express the total form. As an extreme example, an enormous cachepot that sits on the floor would need a massive flower to provide the correct balance. A cachepot with the identical contours, but one that is six inches in diameter, obviously could not support the same flowers.

Don't select a tiny vase and place bulbous tulips in it, although the converse is possible. You can mass many small flowers in an oversized container in order to achieve impact because the flowers are being used as a single element whose total form is overshadowing the singular detail of each flower. This mass of flowers functions in the same way as a field of poppies on a hillside, where the combined effect gives it its strength.

TEXTURE

Texture is always an essential quality in every container. Although we think of texture as alluding to the degree of coarseness on a surface, smoothness is also a texture. An egg has a texture. So does a light bulb. And as you can see, smooth texture can be shiny or matte. And a coarse texture can also be shiny, as a lacquered basket.

Smooth and Rough Surfaces

The smooth-surfaced container in a solid color poses different and more difficult problems than the rough-textured receptacle, which (without any effort on your part)

creates interesting patterns of light and shadow. The smooth vase relates to the flowers as a single shape, and therefore you must supply the means to break up this form by bending branches or a single flower over the side of the container in order to form patterns against the solid outside (drawing of nasturtiums, p. 63).

But there are cases where a smooth finish on a bowl is also broken up by an overall design in the porcelain or ceramic of the container, like a blue-and-white patterned bowl, a flower-painted jardiniere, or the iridescent shadings of an art-nouveau vase (vase, p. 63). Therefore my advice to you is to steer away from smooth, solid, one-color containers because you are immediately confronted with the need to provide additional interest to the container. The plainest container does not offer the easiest solution.

Baskets

One of the great attractions of a basket is that it is such a simple statement of texture, with a myriad of possibilities. People unconsciously gravitate to this subtle detail, not always realizing that it complements many materials—fruits, flowers, nuts, or shells. There are distinct styles of baskets, each with its own personality. Choosing a suitable basket from the incredible variety available will in itself be an exercise for you in deciding which shape, size, color (because there is a tremendous range of color), and texture you would need. Baskets are a whole world unto themselves. I never recommend painting an antique basket, but there are times when a new basket can do the trick if you paint or stain it.

Types of Baskets

Shaker baskets
  simple functional style basket
New England Indian baskets
  stenciled and painted designs (see Plate 11)
Western Indian baskets
  strong geometric forms
Traditional French baskets
  more delicate, formal-style basket (see Plate 22)
Antique Japanese baskets
  extremely imaginative and varied shapes and weaves
  (see Plate 5)
English garden trugs
  simple provincial forms
White wicker baskets
  recalling the Victorian-type flower arrangement

COLOR

Coordinating the colors of the container with the flower arrangement is perhaps the most apparent link between vase and flowers, and can also be the most fun. There is no question that a container splashed with red anemones would be harmonious with a bouquet which repeated the same red anemone. This is true of any painted decoration which can be picked up again in the arrangement.

Colorful geometric or abstract designs on the surface of the pot should also be interlaced in the composition of your flowers (see Plates 19 and 21). A green, viney, trellis-patterned urn suggests the use of twisting vines threaded through the flowers.

Any bands of color on the base or lip of the container add a note of interest and can again be picked up in the flowers.

A salt box contains sprays of bellflowers and sweet peas which flare out from the top, emphasizing the frontal form of the holder.

Japanese baskets come in every shape and weave: *a*, fretted trumpet shape; *b*, square form with fish net pattern of stained bamboo; *c*, vase shaped, with a wide rim, in a closely woven texture; *d*, vertical cylinder in coarse open-work weave; *e*, fat-bellied basket with a narrow neck and a combination of several woven schemes.

f

g

h

i

Western baskets are simpler and more rustic: *f*, laundry basket from Rumania of unpeeled twigs; *g*, South American Indian basket with geometric patterns; *h*, French fruit basket with openwork sides; *i*, American basket of split ash woven in simple design.

Tole containers: *a*, cut out arrow-shape supports encircle the container; *b*, classic vase form with slightly flaring top; *c*, boat-shaped container has an oval form.

All of these details are absorbed by the viewer and he is subconsciously aware of the pleasing total effect of your flower design.

STYLES OF CONTAINERS

You have examined the elements inherent in every container. Now you must combine these four elements in a single object which will be compatible both with the flowers you wish to use and the room in which these flowers are to be placed. Dandelions will never be right in cut crystal, long-stemmed roses won't work in a milk can, nor buttercups in a Grecian urn. The degree of your sensitivity to the qualities expressed in an object, a flower, or a room will be reflected in your work. You must sense the mood; every object brings to mind mental associations, some much more clearly than others. Think of an urn and you immediately see a footed form, classical and formal in feeling. Be alert to your visual images because these ideas will be your best guides. Have confidence in what you instinctively know to be right and you will be starting in a positive way. Don't begin with the attitude that you can compensate in your design for obvious stylistic contradictions. And don't settle for a container just because you happen to have it around.

Once you have your flowers and container in harmony, be careful not to place the arrangement on the wrong piece of furniture. First, the eye must move from the flowers to the container and down to the table. Second, the floral unit must be in balance with the proportions of the furniture where it is resting. You wouldn't put a skinny candle in a big holder, nor would you put a pumpkin on a delicate Regency serving table.

KINDS OF CONTAINERS

ANIMAL FORMS

BASKET SHAPES—(see pages 66 and 67)

BOXES—be careful not to look too contrived
1. tea caddy
2. spice box
3. salt box (drawing, p. 65)
4. window box—best to use plant form or single kind of flower

BUCKET SHAPES
1. brass coal bucket—good for arrangement of greens on floor
2. well bucket—real country look, also for floor or large piece of furniture—needs large mass of flowers
3. porcelain bucket—(see Plate 21)

CACHEPOT (contemporary)—cylindrical form, chrome finish—needs mass of weighty flowers

CACHEPOT (traditional)—most interesting with flowered decoration on it (see Plate 8)

CHINESE JARDINIERE

COMPOTE FORM (usually crystal)—best with hanging-style arrangement

CORNUCOPIA

CROCUS POT AND TULIP VASE—hard to arrange

EPERGNE—a hanging-style arrangement using small delicate flowers is best

FOOD CONTAINERS
1. pitchers
2. dippers
3. old strainers—holes add pattern to flat surface
4. copper pot
5. inverted molds
6. Japanese hibachi

FOOT BATH—charming with large, carefree-style arrangement—needs important location

LAVABO—good way to provide wall interest—use hanging style flower

STONE VESSELS—good in large sizes to create outdoor atmosphere—use with plant forms, branches of leaves, but not complicated arrangements

TOLE CONTAINERS—enormous variety of shapes—lightweight and unbreakable—interesting painted surfaces with provincial designs or marblelized patterns

URNS
1. iron garden urn—good to fill large empty area
2. classic porcelain urn—for formal setting—interesting when used in pairs

VASES
1. Victorian fan-shaped forms in porcelain
2. art-nouveau shapes
3. monochrome oriental style
4. decorated oriental style
5. glass or crystal—best without using filler to secure flowers so as not to detract from the brilliance of the glass

WASHBASIN AND PITCHER—with colorful designs or solid white—a good way to introduce a new container in a bedroom

WOODEN BOWLS—need hefty flower, thick leaves to balance dense wood base

The size or scale of your arrangement is necessarily a part of the location where it is being used. So you must always deal with these two relationships: flowers to container and arrangement to location.

Be artistically demanding. Otherwise you will numb your natural responses and it will become increasingly difficult for you to perceive what is esthetically right. Usually your first response is the most accurate, so heed your initial reaction before you get used to something wrong.

Note: When working with cloth flowers, your choice of containers is unrestricted. You don't have to consider whether your vessel will hold water, nor do you have to concern yourself with putting the arrangement in a container that can be moved in order to change the water. Your receptacle can be anything, anywhere. Its weight, material, and location are not a problem.

6

Putting It Together

It is time to discuss the basic methods you must master to actually make a successful flower arrangement. And yet we should first be aware of one aspect which is unique to the art of flower arranging. In painting and sculpture, the clay, canvas, and paints do not in themselves evoke any particular ideas. They are merely a means of expressing visually the artist's feelings. But in the art of flower arranging you commence by assembling objects that are in themselves perfect and unique. You therefore must contribute a further dimension to the already-established beauty of these single blooms in your flower arrangement. It is in the blending and harmonizing of floral forms that the art of flower arranging is expressed.

The one strikingly important thing which cloth flowers permit, where fresh flowers do not, is that they can be shaped by the arranger to further carry out his artistic design. You may have admired the splendid flower paintings of the Flemish masters, thinking how preoccupied the artist was with the botanical characteristics of each flower. And yet with further study you will discover that many of these painstakingly painted flowers were fantasies of the artist. Not only did he invent his own flowers, but he transformed natural ones into rhythmical pictorial elements in his paintings. He was not self-conscious about mixing spring, summer, fall, and winter flowers in one painted bouquet, because, beyond all else, his goal was to achieve a perfect artistic harmony.

In our discussion now about creating a fabric flower arrangement, remember that you can take the same liberties, for you are not bound by the natural restrictions of a natural flower.

As you proceed to make your arrangement, it is assumed that you have settled in your mind a suitable location, a proper container, and a selection of flowers. You are going to gather together these ingredients and, in stages, build your arrangement.

STAGE 1
FOUNDATION MATERIALS FOR
CLOTH FLOWERS

1. *An Anchoring Material*—styrofoam, which can be cut to fit into any shape of container. It is strong and lightweight, and easily cut.

2. *Sticky Tape Called* Cling—a chewing-gum-like adhesive which anchors the styrofoam to the container. You must just make certain that you put it in the spots where the styrofoam and container make contact.

3. *Floral Clay*—this clay does not dry out and is important to use when the weight of the flowers will topple a lightweight base. You can then weigh down the base with blocks of this floral clay. It is also very helpful when you have a one-sided arrangement and the weight is concentrated in one direction. You can balance the extending flowers by using clay on the opposite side. Clay is also helpful when you wish to fill a very small vase because the clay can be molded to the interior form better than the bulky styrofoam can. The only problem which arises when using clay is that the clay is not able to support heavy stems indefinitely. Since it never hardens, the weight of the flowers eventually causes the flowers to sag.

4. *Sheet Moss*—this is a coarse, natural moss which is available at florists or in the woods, and is used to cover the styrofoam at the top of the container. You have to work the moss around the sides of the styrofoam or clay only if you have a perforated or transparent container, in which case seeing the styrofoam through the sides would be unattractive. The level of the moss should never rise above the level of the container.

Note: Transparent containers do make it difficult to secure the styrofoam and still hide it with the moss because the Cling adhesive does not stick to the moss. The only location where you can put the sticky tape to anchor the styrofoam where it will not be seen is at the very bottom of the container. Filling transparent containers with these securing materials cannot help but detract from the glass because it loses its transparency. So if you feel that a clear container is essential to your particular arrangement, consider arranging the flowers in such a way that the weight and entanglement of the stems will be enough to hold the arrangement together. Even with fresh flowers there are certain limitations when you're dealing with a clear vase. Putting stems that are unattractive and discolor the water quickly in a glass vase should also be avoided. If the stems are to show they must always make a valid design contribution to the whole.

STAGE 2
HOW MANY FLOWERS

You may have already determined what kinds and colors of flowers you are going to use, but you must now decide the quantities of each. An arrangement of twenty cornflowers and two narcissus would be completely different from an arrangement of twenty narcissus and two cornflowers. You must decide which flowers are your filler flowers, which ones will create the overall structure, and which will furnish softening accents. Avoid a one-to-one combination of color because your flowers will look like polka dots if you have an equal number of yellow, blue, and red flowers sprinkled about. If you do work with the same quantities, you can deviate from the spotted effect with knots of color, as you might do with a cluster of pansies inserted into a mass of buttercups. Or you could make undulating bands of color that would work in and out through the arrangement, which is very effectively done with nasturtiums.

Structural Flowers

In an arrangement where the effect is to be carried by the color and form of a large flower, like tulips, you must use enough tulips so that every strong direction that the arrangement takes is carried by the line of a tulip. For example, a three-sided arrangement of tulips placed on a console would have to have at least one tulip to provide the upward thrust, one tulip on each side extending the arms of the arrangement, one or two tulips coming out in the direction of the viewer, and one or more to support the central area. This basic number could be increased in proportion with the size of the arrangement, but no matter how many tulips are added they must, in their positioning, continue to support the established structure.

Filler Flowers

When considering the number of filler flowers or leaves to be used, it is simply a question of using enough to create interest between the large spaces already established by the tulips.

Accent Flowers

The accent flowers again must conform to the strong lines set by the tulips, and bellflowers or other small types of flowers should spring from the lines of the tulips and not create new directions. Therefore there might be a bellflower or columbine fringing the tallest tulips, as well as some of the other tulips.

STAGE 3
COMBINING THE FLOWERS

Tools

For this step you'll need wire, wire cutters, and floral tape.

The gauge of the wire must be heavy enough to support the weight of the flower and not change shape after it has been styled. But it is essential to remember that any additional wire used to lengthen the stem must look like a natural continuance of the stem.

Floral tape is a thin, stretchable material which wraps neatly over the wire and enables you to join flowers as well as to lengthen stems. It is available at florists, comes in green and brown, and the color used should conform with the type of branch you are using.

There is no special kind of clipper, so long as it cuts the wire and is comfortable in your hand. I suggest, when possible, to try out the wire cutter at the hardware store before committing yourself, so you know it can cut what you'll want it to.

Inserting the Flowers

Before inserting the flower you must establish the height, angle, and contour of the flower. So let's go back to a further examination of the frontal arrangement on the console we discussed in Stage 2. Hold the flower over the container at the height you feel will be appropriate in proportion with the base.

Note: If you choose to work in the location where the

PLATE 27

flower arrangement is going to be used, it may be a little messy but safer in the beginning. If you assemble the flowers elsewhere, don't forget decorative elements such as a painting behind the flower arrangement, which will affect the height of the flowers.

Once you have decided on that height, bend the stem and head of the flower so that it will carry the upward emphasis that you want. When choosing your tallest flower, it is very unlikely that you would select one whose head is falling over, as this would contradict the upward sweep (see Plate 8). The two flowers which establish the side thrust also give the arrangement its stability. If they're placed too close to the base of the container, the arrangement may look precarious. If they extend out too far, it may be bottom-heavy. The side extensions also must be different one from the other. The ancient Greek sculptor varied the positions of his models by extending their arms and legs in different poses. So you must extend the arms of your arrangement to create interest. In this situation, one side flower might be bent downward while the one on the other side might curve up.

At this point I must bring to your attention the importance of the angle at which you insert the flower. The top flower was put in with the point going straight down, but you must angle obliquely side flowers so that you get more of a view of the flower head and not its stem.

The front tulips reach out toward the viewer. Their stems should not be too long or they will be in the way. But the angle of the flower must be such that it invites the onlooker into the arrangement.

The central flowers, which provide the necessary bulk to the middle area, should be roughly a third lower than the top flower and the angle at which they are inserted less oblique than that of the side flowers. Obviously the center flowers would not be placed directly in the same line as the front flowers.

With all of these tulips at their different levels you can add greater interest to the group by opening the petals of some and closing others.

Pruning of Flowers

Sometimes it is necessary to prune the stems and branches before inserting them. This is an important way of creating variety. Every stem shouldn't have three flowers, five leaves, and so on. You will want to vary the combinations. The Japanese are particularly self-conscious about the form of every flower they use and are very deliberate when clipping off superfluous leaves and blossoms.

Distribution of Flowers

Spontaneity is the key word to keep in mind when doing a flower arrangement. For as soon as the flowers have a labored self-consciousness they lose the vitality and attraction which makes them such a desirable addition to a room.

It isn't that you should throw the flowers together haphazardly in an effort to achieve a sense of casualness, but guard against reworking and adjusting the flowers so much that they appear to have an invisible net which is restricting their movements. The quick sketch of an artist captures a unique transient quality which can be lost when the drawing is reworked.

Again, we get back to the idea of trusting your initial action. It is that momentary revelation when looking at an object which provides us with insight about that object.

The artist is trained to sustain this awareness during the entire process of creation. And you should learn to hold on to your initial responses and not become limited by your self-criticism.

One of the great attractions in flower arranging is that the possible combinations of flowers and colors are endless, so now when I suggest to you the following possibilities, I am merely trying to illustrate several ideas you should keep in mind.

If you're just going to work with a single kind of flower you might choose sweet peas. Just one color sweet pea is rather uninteresting, even though your object might be to make an arrangement of one color. Take a dozen purple sweet peas, which would look very pretty in a silver-luster jug or a sterling baby's cup. It's not enough just to use this one color. If you only add two blue or pink sweet peas to the twelve, you will supply the needed relief. Your arrangement won't look any less purple, but you will have broken up the solid color mass. The un-ending ocean horizon is relieved by a ship's outline against the infinite space. Two lines on a sheet of colored con-struction paper create design in what would otherwise be formless color. These examples may seem far afield from your simple collection of sweet peas, but it is such an important concept that I feel it cannot be overempha-sized and must never be overlooked, even within the simplest design.

Perhaps you want to put together a combination of narcissus, anemones, and cornflowers. First analyze the proportions. Are the narcissus going to occupy seventy percent of the space, with the anemones and cornflowers utilizing ten percent and twenty percent respectively of the remaining area? If this is your aim, then I would start the arrangement with the narcissus. As a general rule you should always begin your arrangement with the predomi-nating flower or leaf, and proceed successively by intro-ducing the next most plentiful flower, and so on.

This same concept can also be analyzed with the idea of introducing successive levels of flowers in the arrange-ment. The narcissus in your arrangement would be the lowest level, but watch out for creating a perfect dome of flowers. The narcissus have to be staggered up and down, clustered in some spots and airy in others.

Now that you've got the basic rounded structure, you do not want to squeeze the anemones between these flowers, but they should be a little higher than the nar-cissus and rest at a point just above. The interval of space between the height of the narcissus and anemones must be enough to give the anemones freedom, but not so much that you will be aware of a gap between the stages. The cornflowers must also rise above the narcissus and stretch and lighten the feeling of the arrangement. That looseness again harks back to the original thought of creating a feeling of spontaneity, and I utilize every means in an effort to create a free-flowing arrangement. My favorite is the introduction of wisps of grass. I also love the ten-drils on the sweet peas which shoot out and relieve what might otherwise be too heavy a shape. Buds on roses and peonies, and spiraling sedum are all important aids.

A grand assortment of delphiniums, stock, lilacs, lilies, carnations, and peonies needs a base of leaves to balance the large proportions of the flowers. Imagine that you wish to make this arrangement for the circular table that sits at the far end of your living room. Although people don't usually walk behind this table, it is still free-standing in the room and I would therefore advise you to make an "all around" arrangement—one that can be seen from all sides, as opposed to a "frontal" arrangement. The object with such a diversified assortment of blooms is not to choose too many flowers of one variety. If you're working with a cachepot that measures twelve inches in height by nine inches in diameter, five delphiniums, three stock, eight liliums, five peonies, and ten carnations should be a good balance. But all of these flowers will be introduced to the structure which you will initially outline with branches of leaves. The peony might be introduced first because it is larger than all the other flowers, and therefore you must be sure to allow sufficient space around each flower and to vary the attitude and stem shape. The lilies are next, and their pointed petals are interesting when juxtaposed with the thick peony head. The lilacs are also large flowers, but they don't have the density of the peony. Their dark green leaves and clustered buds offer another texture to the arrangement. The vertical thrust of the majestic delphinium relieves what might be too heavy an assortment. The stock, in a less dramatic way, offers another vertical line. And finally, among all of these glorious flowers, the very graceful arc-shaped stem of the carnation is another means of lightening the look.

When you put your arrangement together, you are forced to create a sense of freedom in the arrangement itself. You do not have the advantages of the painter, who can so effectively create a sense of ease by the addition of a fallen petal or a tumbled flower on a tabletop.

Take advantage of every device to engender a feeling of freshness in all your arrangements, whether you use real flowers or artificial.

The foxglove stalk with feltlike trumpets adds elegance and height.

7

Outlining It All

The outcome of every arrangement has three possible results—poor, passable, and perfect. And, it seems to me, if you appraise the needs of your arrangement carefully, the results will be right. It is now time for us to break down the setting and analyze each contributing element.

Let me interject at this time that for an arrangement to be perfect in its setting does not mean that it is necessarily the outstanding object in the room.

Are you able to describe in words the mood of your living room? Before I ask anyone what the style of their decor is, I first try to ascertain the mood which they are endeavoring to achieve. A living room with Chinese Chippendale furniture could be stark and severe if those dark furniture shapes were placed against white walls. The same style Chippendale furniture could have soft needlepoint seat coverings and be placed in a room with peach silk walls. You would still have a decorative setting of English furniture, but the emotional response to each of these rooms would be completely different. If you cannot describe the aura which you are trying to convey in your interior design, then you had better forget about flowers for the time being, and go back and reappraise your decoration. A flower arrangement cannot hope to express in a room a look which has not already been established.

Room Moods

One sure way to create a dominant effect in your room is to select a distinctive patterned material which can be carried out in your drapery fabric, chair coverings, and even on the walls. This is perhaps the easiest way to unify a setting, just as you can most easily coordinate a black dress with black shoes and a black bag. Because it is one of the easiest methods of organizing a decorative scheme, it also requires the proper sense of restraint in selecting the areas which should use the same material. The patterns of these materials could be anything: checks, stripes, plaids, small florals, large florals, toiles, geometrics, etc. When a dominant print of this kind is used, it is simple to repeat the same mixture of color in your flower arrangement. With the vast choice of patterned fabrics available to you, you could achieve the gamut of decorative effects. Think for a moment how different the effect of pink-and-white gingham walls and curtains would be compared to a coarse brown-and-white houndstooth. Even if both these fabrics were used to cover the same areas in identical rooms, the resulting effect could in no way be the same. And so the pattern you choose is the bud from which the total room design should flower.

And in this way every addition you make to this setting must be a further expression of the original look created by your fabric pattern.

The primary reason for unsuccessful interior decoration is that most people start without having any preconceived objective, and they therefore assemble disparate objects. You can't get dressed in the morning unless you have some idea how you want to look—tweedy, frilly, or like a farmer. It all has to hang together Therefore, the person who is unable to describe the direction of his room has a room that is suffering from a lack of planning.

Unfortunately, this is not always your own fault, for most people start their decoration with hand-me-downs and try diligently to achieve a cohesive look with incompatible pieces. It's hard to advise anyone when they are faced with this dilemma. However, if your dowry contains a variety of kinds of furniture, try somehow to select, as a nucleus for your room, one piece that has a distinctive and desirable style, whether it be a ladderback rocker, an ebony piano, or a comfortable Lawson sofa. You have to keep blinders on because today, more than ever, the incredible variety of objects, wallpapers, fabrics, and furniture can be so distracting that you are constantly waylaid by exciting designs which may have no relation to the style of your room. If you succumb to the myriad temptations, you will either have to have a different home for every look that you admire, or you'll end up with one room looking like a Turkish bath while another resembles a French salon.

Now let us imagine that you are proceeding in a most organized manner to establish a look in your room. There are countless possibilities, but perhaps the enumeration of a few will give you the idea of what I mean.

You must first analyze the physical restrictions of the room. Is it large or small? Bright or dark? With high ceilings or low ceilings? Are there large stretches of wall, or are most of the walls broken by door and window openings? All of these factors must condition your choice of decor. The scale of your furniture and the designs in the fabrics or wallpaper must be balanced with the proportions of the overall setting.

You must then unite these physical conditions with your personal feelings, for you must be able to determine the type of setting in which you will feel most comfortable.

You will find in the following outline the basic elements representative of many styles of decor. Any combination of the following characteristics will enable you to achieve the feeling of a specific style.

ENGLISH COUNTRY

Furniture
Welsh dressers
gateleg tables
Windsor chairs
wing chairs
trestle tables
settles
hutches

Floor Coverings
plank floors
painted and stenciled floors
oriental rugs
hooked and braided rugs

Fabrics
crewel designs
traditional floral patterns
hopsacking
leather
corduroy
linens

Containers
pitchers
colorful ironstone
country baskets
brass, copper, and steel
foot baths
buckets

TRADITIONAL ENGLISH

Furniture
Chippendale
Sheraton
Queen Anne
Regency
wing chairs
camelback sofas
tea tables
highboys
lowboys
candlestands

Fabrics, Floors, and Floor Coverings
damasks
velvets
polished wood floors
oriental rugs

Accessories and Fixtures
swags and tie-back curtains
pier mirrors
gilt frames
crystal and brass lighting
   fixtures

Containers
porcelain cachepots
urns
epergnes
crocus pots
hunt bowls

FRENCH COUNTRY

Furniture
fruitwoods
Louis XV style
Louis XVI style
armoires
skirted tables
bouillotte lamps
pleated lamp shades

Fabrics and Floor Coverings
small flower prints
striped fabrics and ticking
floral rugs and needlepoint

Containers
decorated faience
toleware
French fretted baskets

CONTEMPORARY

Furniture, Fabrics, and Floor Coverings
glass and steel furniture
leather and tweed upholstery
woven decorative panels
bold prints and weaves
tile flooring
dark stained floors
shag rugs

Containers
chrome containers
pottery jugs and bowls
woven rush baskets

CHINESE DECORATION

Furniture
Chinese-inspired
lacquer
bamboo
Chinese dower chests

Colors
cinnabar red
black
celadon green
lapis lazuli blue
persimmon

Fabrics, Floor Coverings, and Accessories
chinoiserie-design fabrics
raw silks
Chinese rugs
oriental sculptures
screens and oriental panels

Containers
oriental baskets
simple monochromatic vases
multicolor Chinese ginger jars

blue and white Chinese
porcelains
lacquerware

AMERICAN COUNTRY

Furniture
pine and maple woods
benches
spool beds
ladder-back chairs
rocking chairs
corner cupboards

Colors
pumpkin
rust
ocher
sea-foam green
cranberry
slate blue

Fabrics and Accessories
small prints
hopsacking
quilts
samplers and primitive
    paintings
brick and wood trim

Containers
woodenware
copperware and tinware
brass tubs
crockery pitchers
Indian baskets

BEACH HOUSE LOOK

Furniture
rattan
wicker
bamboo
comfortable overstuffed chairs
    in cotton fabrics

Colors
yellows
greens
whites

*Fabrics, Floors, and Floor
Coverings*
bright cotton prints
painted floors
canvas and sailcloth coverings
hemp and sisal floor coverings
textured carpeting

Containers
colorful ceramic cachepots
clay pots
wicker baskets
hanging baskets
lavabos

Now that you have clearly established, both for your-self and for the visitor, an ambience, or look, in every room, you can consider your flowers.

You might even try out your effect by asking a friend for his immediate response. How does a room strike him—calming, warm, or cozy? Let's leave this point with the hope that you have accepted its premise, and that now you will be able to survey the areas of your home with the idea of determining where a flower arrangement would be most appropriate.

As your eye scans the space, you will notice voids where additional interest and color are needed. There's a very big difference between an empty space and a void, and you must look at the shapes in your room in the same way you would examine a painting so as not to mistake an open area, with an important shape of its own, for a dull area that creates no interest. The bareness of one part of a room adds intensity and strength to another area, which might combine many decorative elements. Look for the voids, and determine whether you want to make them focal points, color highlights, or space fillers.

These three possibilities will help you to determine the appropriate type of flower. It is unlikely that you would use a large, brilliant flower in an arrangement which you wanted to recede into the background.

Space Filler

I think the arrangement that occupies this secondary position in the room is more difficult to select than one which is to be the most prominent. There is always the danger of it being too drab or too strong, and to strike a happy balance requires restraint.

Take, for example, a small pottery container with a

blue/red glaze, filled with a handful of rust and purple sweet peas. This is placed on one of a pair of end tables that flank a dramatic camelback sofa. On each table is a large Imari vase made into a lamp, and this small pot of flowers, which picks up the coloring in the Japanese porcelains, is a simple means of varying the identical side tables. I don't think the flowers themselves are even noticed, but they provide the relief in a repetitive furniture arrangement.

Looking at this sofa area, which dominates the room, it is evident that this type of filler arrangement is all that's needed. Anything more would have detracted from the effect of the highly decorated vases and the sofa.

Color Accent

With the great interest in colorful printed materials and wallpapers, you are left with the job of choosing one color from the combination of colors in your fabric. You can individualize the fabric by the colors you choose to stress. And sometimes utilizing for your arrangement a color which plays a minor part in the overall fabric scheme can create a much more subtle and perceptive flower arrangement than one which is an obvious repeat of the most prominent colors of the fabric. It is important to awaken the eye to the numerous color qualities in a combination rather than copying the obvious ones so much that the other interest is smothered.

When you try to accent the colors in your room, don't fall into the trap of choosing the most obvious color. A midnight-blue fabric with geranium-red patterns would not be any more interesting if you chose the same geranium red for your flower arrangement. But that fabric might really come alive if you combined the geranium

hue with a fuchsia or with heliotrope tones. This rule of thumb will assist you in your choice of color for an arrangement that is intended to supply a color highlight.

Focal Point

Focal point does mean where your eye is drawn. This is done by the way in which the furniture is arranged and color areas are introduced. You cannot artificially create a focal point where it does not exist because you cannot intellectually condition a person's eye to rest on a spot unless many decorative elements have established the importance of that spot.

A wall curtained with the most vivid fabric may lead the eye to a small empty tabletop. It is not the size of the space which necessarily determines its focal importance, nor is it the brightness of color. Think of a drawing which shows a succession of arc-shaped lines. The eye is naturally drawn to the spot from which the lines radiate. Two important upholstered couches on either side of a mantel direct the eye to focus on the mantel.

It may be more difficult for you, as the designer of your room, to determine its focal point. You may wish to emphasize a location that is not naturally the most obvious because you may be confusing an empty area with the focal point. So endeavor to look impartially at the scheme you have constructed. It is not as difficult as it might sound, since most rooms combine basic furniture groupings. For example, a coffee table in front of a sofa, a table between two windows, a table in front of a large window, end tables, dining room table with chairs, etc.

If any one of these critical locations lacks sufficient decorative interest, this is where you must place your flower arrangement.

PLATE 28

Seasonal Decorations

Seasonal decorations are a further extension of your decor. Don't try to harmonize gingham with lucite. If you try to create a whole new look within an already established atmosphere, you will work twice as hard and be half as successful. Always work with what you've got. Don't fight it.

If you're having a party at a time when there is no particular seasonal association, don't suddenly introduce red roses if your room looks best with yellow tulips. When decorating for a party it is dangerous to feel that you must surprise everyone with a whole new look in your home. But if you really want to have a beautiful party, and not one that will just shock the guests with its novelty, work on enhancing what you have.

I think the most festive thing you can do with flowers is to have an abundance of them. Greet your guests with flowers as they first walk in by placing an array on your elevator landing or front steps. Masses of daisies in a tub are delightful, fresh, and festive. If they are cloth daisies, you have the advantage of buying them once and reusing them.

Entrance-hall tables and buffet tables welcome your guests when they are massed with flowers in baskets or bowls. The effect is much stronger than if you were to scatter a few flowers in many locations. In this case, put all your eggs in one basket, and create a smashing arrangement.

The Care of Cloth Flowers

Let's be practical. If you evaluate the merit of cloth flowers from an economic point of view, they will test very high. The initial investment, when working with cloth flowers, is much greater than that with fresh flowers. However, it quickly evaporates after a short period of time. If there were a location in your home where you wished to have a permanent arrangement of anemones, supplying the necessary fresh flowers weekly is a far more costly method than arranging cloth anemones for the location, which would remain an attractive asset for a couple of years.

When you have worked with cloth flowers, the convenience of having flowers at all times in your home permits last-minute parties to be uncomplicated with the additional chore of buying and arranging fresh flowers. Having beautiful fabric flower arrangements around, whether anyone is coming or not, is also a pleasure one lives without when one is constantly having to buy fresh flowers.

I can't dispute the joy of cutting flowers from your own garden for your home, but no matter how bountiful your garden is, it has its seasonal limitations. There is no question that having worked with real flowers, you have a better understanding of how to handle cloth flowers, not so much in the way the flowers are manipulated, but rather in an overall understanding of the properties and characteristics that flowers embody.

If someone asked you to imitate or describe something, the better your acquaintance with this object or idea, the more expressive your interpretation would be. So I encourage you to explore and enjoy flowers wherever you can because all of these impressions will enlarge your feelings for flowers and will permit you to make more successful arrangements with greater ease. You cannot fully appreciate a caricature of a person unless you have some knowledge of that person.

Of course, all the practical reasons for having flowers in your home are applicable to businesses. Perhaps even more so, since few organizations are staffed with people who have sufficient time or interest to concern themselves with the correct decorative accessories in a reception room, showroom, lobby, bank, etc.

The best way to maintain cloth flowers is to handle them as little as possible once they are put in place in an arrangement. The stems and leaves are all wired and can be easily rearranged if they are bent out of place. The petals of many flowers are also wired, permitting them to be opened or closed easily. Some of these flowers are liliums, tulips, and clematises. But you must bear in mind that cloth flowers will fray and deteriorate if they are brushed and handled continually. Therefore, when cleaning them it is best to flick off surface dust with your finger. You could use a dry cloth to wipe off dust on broad, flat leaves, but it is not advisable to vacuum or brush the flowers since this will only increase the wear.

Also, if the flowers have drooped, a little careful and patient reshaping will work. Steaming the flowers is not advisable in most cases, as it usually makes the flowers more limp and often dissolves the glue that is used in assembling some flowers.

Cloth flowers are assembled with a combination of fine wire, glue, and floral tape. Sometimes rubber tubing is used to cover the stem wire. But whatever the kind of flower, these basic materials are applied.

The only other precaution you can take to preserve your bouquet is to cover it lightly with a thin piece of plastic when you go away, and to keep it out of sunny areas as much as possible.

The vivid opaque
petaled anemone has
a black button center
and tubular stem
that can be twisted
into interesting
shapes.

8

The Anemone Woman

Does Jean Harlow remind you of a gardenia . . . Joan Crawford of deep red carnations? Characterizing a person in terms of a flower isn't something new. The too-hackneyed expression about the "long-stemmed beauty" is one we all know. If you think about it, at some time you have probably associated many familiar personalities with certain flowers. The people we find most interesting are those with strong individual characteristics which set them apart. They usually maintain their individuality amid the fluctuations of style, and this is basically what makes them attractive to us.

The charm of Audrey Hepburn is somehow expressed by the lily of the valley, and no matter what, Elizabeth Taylor will always be a velvety red rose. Hedy Lamarr is orchidness. And Jane Fonda is that most contemporary flower, the anemone. She has a directness like the vivid hues of the petals, the sleekness and streamlines of the sinuous stem.

To take this concept a step further and translate an individual's personal attributes into the very distinctive characteristics of a flower requires empathy rather than superficiality. We all have very definite associations attached to flowers and I'm sure you can think of many people you know who bring to mind specific flowers.

Countless poets have supplied us with musings about the nature of flowers. Painters have contributed their visual interpretations. And history has reaffirmed the association of certain flowers with stylistic trends. The papyrus, with its simple form, conveys the severity and strength characteristic of Egyptian art (drawing, p. 90).

Papyrus is the plant form most often found in ancient Egyptian art.

And so it's no accident that today so many women tell me their favorite flower is the anemone. Since the anemone typifies the woman of the 1970s, it follows that it will be appropriate in her home, as well as directly related to her fashion sense. After all, the home of the '70s has a flowing line, boldness of color, and the use of organic forms as opposed to geometric shapes. Contour seats shaped to the body and the undulating line which predominates in patterns are both reminiscent of the anemone. In this environment, the unstructured, braless woman is perfectly in tune with her emancipated setting.

But you don't have to be an anemone woman. Although the anemone is the single flower which I think represents the times better than any other, there are countless choices which are valid. The most important thing is to perceive your personal preferences and not become muddled by current styles with which the media is bombarding you. Choosing your own flowers is a superb opportunity to express your taste, for in a world which daily presents a multitude of "things," the act of selection is creative. It's encouraging to me to find a widespread interest in making something yourself. I'm always happy when someone prefers buying my flowers loose so he can participate in the design of the finished product, imparting his own uniqueness. The more you work with flowers, the more agile and adept you will become in handling them, and the better your results.

The constant fluctuations in stylistic trends add to the confusion and make it more difficult for the individual to be discriminating about his own needs. No sooner do you think you have settled upon an appropriate look for you than your confidence is shattered by a new fad. So make sure when you are evaluating your artistic requirements (for flowers or anything else) that you are aware of what is really a significant direction rather than another dead end.

Not too long ago, in the Jackie Kennedy era of the 1960s, the daisy was up front in flower popularity. It was fresh, clean, and direct, but without the sophistication of the anemone. Fashions were just beginning to express greater freedom and homes everywhere seemed to be in shades of sunny yellow with its constant companion, the green-and-white print. Wicker was wonderful and everything was bright and airy.

The "daisy lady" will always be with us, with her accompanying style of decor. And this is good, since I think the object in fashion and interior design, as I have said, is to establish for yourself what's most becoming and stick to it no matter how fashion evolves. As you can see, there is a way of being selective in both fashion and home furnishings so that you are not forced to adulterate your best look. It's the person who swings from one look to another who never achieves any style. We've all seen the woman who sports the current fashion symbols and we immediately recognize the lack of discrimination with which they have been chosen. But it is much more difficult to appraise yourself. Perhaps you're most at ease in an eighteenth century setting and you favor the lushness of roses and pale hues of delphiniums and lilacs. Or are you a Victorian throwback who loves the involvement of many objects, the deep, rich crimsons and golds, and thick little nosegays of violets, sweet william, and mignonettes. That's fine, and don't let anyone talk you out of it. The perceptive interior designer is one who strains out these qualities and fulfills for you the appropriate ambience. Too many people have lived in French country decor with French country flowers like poppies and marguerites when they really might

have been more at ease on a southern plantation with boughs of magnolias and gigantic peonies.

The Japanese are an example of misguided design when they abandon their own innate style to follow a western look. Though they are enraptured with roses, their attempts to use them are always disastrous. In Japan when I see rose-patterned brocades and floral arrangements of roses I am saddened since I know that the same effort when directed to their own kind of flower would be superb. Somehow Japanese people think that westerners want to see western things, and the first thing the Japanese flower maker shows me is always a rose, which they think is beautiful and which I usually find leaden and ugly. However, the most magnificent cloth iris I have ever seen was made for me by the Imperial Flower Maker to the Emperor of Japan and this flower is an example of Japanese design at its best.

Have we, without realizing it, established that a flower, more than any object, can symbolize fashion and decorating trends, and even the magnitude of a country? The fleur-de-lis at once suggests France. The thistle connotes Scotland. The rose of England evolved to later represent, in white, the Yorkists and, in red, the Lancastrians. The marriage of Henry Tudor to Eleanor of York was figuratively represented by the union of the red rose with the white.

Our acceptance of specific flowers for specific historical periods has been most clearly illustrated by the flower painters of those times, who truly sensed the appropriateness of certain blooms. When thinking of the Flemish school, the tulip is paramount. It was of commercial importance, since great fortunes were made in the tulip-bulb business, and its linear quality and definite color was much

Stately flowers on
their tapering stems
and boughs of
flowers add height
and importance—
delphinium, lilac,
hollyhock, stock.

enjoyed by the artists, who recorded it in the most marvelous undulating shapes.

For eighteenth century France we have been schooled to envision a much fuller floral mass, from the gigantic bouquets of roses, snapdragons, and lilies of the valley that must have perfumed the gilded palace chambers. The shades of flowers also fall mainly into the paler tones of rose, yellow, mauve, and blue. And even in the nineteenth century, with Renoir, there is still that same color quality and profusion. When I visit Paris in the spring I am always charmed by the abundance of pink, purple, and blue hydrangeas everywhere.

The English are the great gardeners of the world, and their attitude toward flowers has always seemed to me to be studious. I think of the many fantastic books on botany, dating back to the fifteenth and sixteenth centuries, which illustrate in the minutest detail hundreds of flowers and herbs. In England, the style of arranging is grand in scale, with a stately quality very much at home with Chippendale and Sheraton. Stock, foxglove, hollyhock, and flowers with this imposing look always stud the periphery of the arrangement, and phlox, sweet william, and roses are massed at the center (drawing, p. 92). There are many charming churches that dot the English countryside and when you enter you always find this kind of array near the altar.

There is a wild abandon which has always been characteristic of the Italian flower style. Their gardens are a tangle of vines, sometimes falling from great stone urns, with pinks and poppies and bellflowers intermixed, cascading fountains, and statues. All the flowers are related to an architectural setting. This alliance lends an air of baroque magnificence. At a villa I visited outside of Florence, even the simple geranium was transformed into the most grandiose of flowers. Great stone pots were toppling with these fantastic blooms which had taken over the entire enclosure.

In the East, the Japanese garden is supreme in contrasting the delicate colorings and textures of plants. The most esoteric gardens I have ever seen are at Katsura in Kyoto, formerly an imperial residence. Hundreds of varieties of mosses and ground covers are subtly blended. Everything is restrained and calculated to perfection. Within the Japanese home the flower arrangement also plays upon the nuances of form, and on its symbolic import. Of course you cannot forget the chrysanthemum, which above all flowers is characteristic of Japan, for the sixteen-petaled chrysanthemum represents the emperor. In the East, the single flower is treated with the utmost respect, since one perfect flower is a more satisfying accomplishment than a mass of imperfect ones. I can't help but think of the countless pots in front of Japanese homes nurturing one magnificent chrysanthemum.

Chinese floral designs are more opulent and the heavy blossoms of the magnolia and peony are strongly Chinese. The tradition of flower arranging is very old in China and was an important part of both religious and domestic life. And even in our western flower arrangements we constantly make use of the marvelous Chinese floral-decorated porcelains. In my own home, against a Chien Lung wall painting of a flowering magnolia tree, I have placed a selection of giant peonies (Plate 15).

I guess the most American flower is the daisy, and close behind comes the black-eyed susan. And these are so appropriate in the direct, informal style of the American arrangement, which is always charming in an ironstone pitcher or colorful foot bath. The orangey tones of zin-

A simple pottery vase is appropriate for the casual daisy. The loose arrangement stresses the upward thrust of the container form.

nias, marigolds, and tiger lilies, and the brightness of buttercups and ranunculas, all complement the maple and pine woods used in American furniture. The colors of these flowers also blend with natural basket materials, homespun and rural accessories. Perhaps it is our traditional instincts and our love of a warm and cozy environment which leads so many of my customers to select these shades for their homes.

Countries, fashions, and interiors have their flowers. Now, your vocabulary of flowers should permit you to express in your own home the most suitable type of arrangement.

List of Suppliers

Alexander King at Garfinckle's (Washington, D.C.)

Burdines (Miami, Orlando, West Palm Beach, Fort Lauderdale, Pompano, Hollywood)

Diane Love, Inc. (851 Madison Avenue, New York, N.Y. 10021)

I. Magnin (Los Angeles, Seattle, Portland, Sacramento)

May D. & F. (Denver)

Wells Design (1801 South Post Oak Road, Houston, Texas 77027)

For additional shopping information, please contact:
  Diane Love, Inc.
  851 Madison Avenue, New York, N.Y. 10021 (212) 879-6997.

Index

transparent, 72
white, 56
Contemporary decor, 81
Cornucopia, 69
Crocus pot, 69

Daisy, popularity of (1960s), 91
Dining room, flower arrangement in, 43, 45
Dried flowers, 3

English country decor, 81
English flower style, 91, 93
Entrance hall, flower arrangement in, 29–30
Epergne, 69

Fabric flowers
    advantages of, 4, 8, 11, 71–72
    and arrangement framework, 17
    care of, 86–87
    containers for, 70
    economy of, 86
    evolution of, 4
    foundation materials for, 72
    functions of, 73
    number of, 72–73
    opportunities for, 7–8
    and window location, 37–38
    See also Flowers
Floral clay, 72
Floral tape, 73
Florists, and standardized flower arrangements, 2–3
Flower arrangements
    "all around" vs. "frontal," 77–78
    artistry of, 8, 14, 17, 71
    in bedroom, 45
    boundaries of, 17
    color in, 18, 20, 23
    as color accent, 83

color combinations in, 51, 53–54
commercial, 2–3
containers for, 59, 61–62, 64–65, 68–70
contour in, 23
density in, 23
in dining room, 43, 45
dominant and subordinate locations for, 37
in entrance hall, 29–30
flower forms in, 27
as focal point, 83
levels in, 77
in living room, 30, 32, 34, 37–38
multishaded flowers in, 54
and room mood, 79
and room unification, 50–51
scale in, 13, 14
sculptural qualities in, 14, 17, 18
as seasonal decoration, 86
selecting colors for, 47–48, 50–51, 53–54, 56
shapes in, 17–18
as space filler, 82–83
stages in, 72–73, 76–78
texture in, 27
See also Fabric flowers; Flowers
Flowers
    accent, 73
    distribution of, 76–78
    filler, 73
    importance of, 11
    insertion of, 73, 76
    and personality, 89
    pruning of, 76
    structural, 73
    stylistic trends in, 90–91
    symbolism of, 91
    universality of, 1
    and window location, 37
    See also Fabric flowers